LOVE HAS SOMETHING TO SAY

LOVE HAS SOMETHING TO SAY

LOVE HAS SOMETHING TO SAY

DOROTHY LOVE

Library of Congress Control Number: 2017900620
ISBN: Hardcover   978-1-5245-7672-1
                Softcover   978-1-5245-7671-4
                eBook   978-1-5245-7670-7

Edited by Linnie Bradley and Tori Dismuke, Wendy Ryals Horne and Robert Stewart (grandson)

Print information available on the last page.

Rev. date: 02/03/2017

To order additional copies of this book, contact:
Xlibris
1-888-795-4274
www.Xlibris.com
Orders@Xlibris.com
749072

CONTENTS

Waldo, Arkansas

Some hundreds of years ago is when and how this family got started, the real beginning, when Frank Messer proposed and married Molly Mixon my great grandparents.

Left: Their home

Bottom Left:
Molly and Frank Messer

Bottom Right:
New Bethel A.M.E.
Church of Waldo

Acknowledgement

Jacquelyn Brewer for the confidence you gave me when I started to get a little weary because I had not gotten any response from the one hundred query letters I had sent to various publishers. You reminded me that I was a child of God and he was still in control. Thanks for all the financial help you and your husband Charles gave me.

Diane Rene, for all the typing you did. Even though you did not feel well, you pressed on to help me finish.

Mary Bax, for all the typing of labels for companies that I needed to mail queries to.

Yvonne Williams, a family friend and girlfriend of my Brother, for the gift of supplies.

R.C. and Ceclia Burch, for the many nights they let me crash over at their house so that I did not have to drive home to Corona.

Birdie, a nurse at the hospital where my daughter Regina had surgery, for taking such good extra care of her.

All my children for supporting and believing in their Mom.

To Aunt Rossie for all your encouragement and positive input, regarding me writing this book.

To my cousin Maudie, thank you a thousand times my cousin, my friend, for allowing me to stay at your home. For your prayers, encouragement, tears of joy and your positive input in the completion of my book. Your loyal love and support go beyond a cousin. It is kind and genuine. When I would get tired and bewildered, you would help me get through the day with prayer and words of encouragement. Many days as I was leaving your home you would hear me call out to the Lord, Lord how long, and the Lord would use your voice I do believe, to say not long. Guess what? I made it. I love you.

To my cousin Connie for your encouragement and quick thinking. I expressed to you I needed a release letter, to mail everyone. Five minutes later it was done.

To my daughter Deborah for calling to tell me how proud she was of me for writing and finishing my book, and to have me for a mom.

To my goddaughter, Wendy, for allowing me to fill in the gap for her mom, for believing in me, giving me compliments, much needed love, financial support, and prayers. Also to my godson, her husband Willie, for his support and prayers.

Much and many thanks to you, Gracie Davis, for your support and your encouragement during the completion of my book—one of the best and understanding supervisors I've ever had. "More on Gracie in Book Two."

Two special young ladies at ImPress (OfficeMax, Incorporated) made this publication possible. Many thanks and appreciation to Amara Poolswasdi (cover design, editorial design, typesetting), and Parisa Alimi for her patience and cooperation. Also to a special young man, Joseph King. Your team made it happen for me and I am grateful.

To a special guy, "London Easley," my no. 1 fan for all the encouragement and push to keep pressing on to the finish line. For being such a wonderful listener, for all of this I truly thank you. Thank you also for love, support, and friendship.

To my friend, Lois Easley, for being overjoyed and happy for me writing this book, from the first day I told you about it. For your positive input and encouragement. Much love and thanks to you and your husband Marvin for your support and for calling me sis.

Thank you Catherine Kennard for your prayers and support, for all your suggestions as to how to promote my book. Also, for your wonderful enthusiasm for me writing a book. Just for being my friend.

Of all of the Thank You's, my book would not have been completed without this special thank you.

To my wonderful, beautiful sister Maxine; to my superb, handsome, and witty brother William; this is your book, my book, our book that could have never ever been written without you. This book is "our" life story: it tells all. We've been through the storm. We've had some good days. We've had some hills to climb, but as I look around and think things over, we won't complain, who knows the story any better than God?

Thank you my sister, thank you my brother forbeing a part of me, for being a part of my life.

I love you, I love you, I love you.

I am sorry, but to actually mention every name of the people that are worthy of Thank You's would take up many, many more pages. Perhaps you said a prayer, or gave a sincere smile, or a "You Go Girl" gesture, I'm grateful. I thank you.

You are acknowledged in my heart.

Author's Note

Many thanks first of all to God Almighty, who is the head of my life; for giving me the strength, courage, wisdom and knowledge to write this book; for the healing that has already started in our lives. Again, I say if it had not been for the Lord on our side, where would we be?

It has not been my intention to hurt, embarrass, humiliate, intimidate, or anger anyone in the writing of this book. This is the true story of my life, positive and negative situations.

Foreword

This is an autobiography of my life story. This book will reveal how three small children survived the brutal murder of their mother and two- year old sister. It was my four-year old brother who discovered their bodies lying lifeless in pools of blood and saw the assailant running from the scene. Raised by our grandmother (who was very religious) she never felt the need to seek professional counseling to help us through our emotional traumatic experience. Love Has Something To Say is an in depth story of my personal encounter with the trials, tribulations and struggles that I had to endure throughout my life; pushed into the role of mama, sister, friend and decision maker. Being labeled the boss, the strong one, was a very hard and heavy burden that sometimes took its toll on me. It also depicts how my relatives, friends, and extended family helped my siblings and me overcome life's despair. This book also demonstrates how you can bear the grief and pain of life with the love and support of God and everyone else who loves you.

This is why I have something to say.

Indeed this book has been a long time coming. I knew I had to tellsomeone about my hurt and pain that I had been feeling for as long as Ican remember, at least fifty years. I kept thinking to myself, who do I tell? How do I begin telling what happened that day? Who will listen and whocares? This sort of thing happens all over the world everyday. One day ithit me. Write it! Write a book and name it, "Love Has Something to Say." The hope is that this will bring some closure to the three of us or anyoneelse who has ever lost a loved one so tragically.

THE BEGINNING

WHAT ever happened to the four-year old boy who just wanted to run home for a minute to check on and say hello to his mother and little sister? He had gone earlier to play at a neighbor's home for an hour. Mother and two year old sister Joyce were going to take a nap. He had been told by his mother to be home in a couple of hours because we all were going out for dinner.

What he found would haunt him for the rest of his life. It was a horror scene from hell. Confused and scared, he ran out of the house crying and screaming for help. The perpetrator, still in the house, ran out the back door into the woods, making one mistake: he looked back.

Who did the little boy see? He was petrified. This face would haunt him for the rest of his life.

Love Has Something to Say, June 17, 1996

Again, giving honor and all praises to God who is the head of my life; God's grace and mercy have brought me through, and I have something to say.

Some of the names in this book have been changed or altered to protect various people and to protect myself. This book is dedicated to my lovely family, my loyal and faithful friends, old and new. I love you.

I was born Dorothy Jean Love, April 26, 1940 in Waldo, Arkansas, or so I was told. Records of my birth have not been found. I was delivered by a midwife, Bertha Love, my grandmother. I was the second of five children born to Willie and Lorene Love.

To my sister, Maxine Love and my brother, William Love, we made it. The three of us know that if it had not been for the Lord on our side, where would we be?

To my children, Pamela Reeves, Regina Reeves Cole, Deborah Reeves, and Gregory Spencer, you are my everything, you are my life. Thank you for hanging in there with me. We have had many ups and downs, and sometimes you felt as if I was not there for you, that I was too strict and didn't understand. I was there all the time praying and trusting in God. Some of my words or actions were hard or harsh at times, but I had my reasons for whatever was said or done. Forgive me if I was misunderstood; understand that I was a young, single mother raising four children, doing the best I could the only way I knew how. Sometimes I was too hard on you girls and too soft and protective of my son. I wanted all of you to be strong, independent, respectful and to love each other. I made mistakes, and some wrong decisions. We have come a long way. The key words love and togetherness. I thank God Almighty that we made it. You are my joy, my sadness, my anger and, believe it or not, my four best friends.

To all of my wonderful, beautiful grandchildren, I am so grateful to your parents for having you; you're irreplaceable, I love you all.

Sit back, and get comfortable, for we must know the past before we journey to the future.

Below: Mother and baby Joyce

Chapter I

MOTHER

Above: Cousin Jerline
Below: Cousins Rosy and Rossie

Mother was a soft-spoken, easy-going lady. Yes, lady. She was special to everyone. I am remembering a petite, fair complexioned, long haired, beautiful woman with a wonderful sincere spirit, full of life. She was always trying to figure things out: what will I feed my children for dinner today, and what about tomorrow, what will they wear to keep warm? She was constantly worrying, not smiling much at all. She had the saddest eyes I've ever seen, telling so much, even when she was smiling. I don't ever remember seeing her happy. Mother, so young, and yet so lonely. Her life was taken from her at an early age. She was twenty-four years old.

Mother had a half-sister that she loved very much. They would talk as often as possible. Dorothy Faye was still in school and would come to visit her sister on the weekend. She called Mother Sis, having a lot of respect and love for her older sister. When mother was murdered, Aunt Dorothy Faye was devastated. She stated that she would never get over this murder of her sister and niece. She felt guilty for not being there more often or for not doing more for her. How could anyone do this to a little innocent baby who is such a wonderful person, loved by every one that knew and met her?

Mother hated spanking her children. If she had to chastise us, she would cry too. When it was my turn to get a spanking, I would run and get under the house. I don't know how much room there was from the house to the ground, but I managed to get under there screaming and crying. I could always get to that porch and down under I would go, praying as loud as I could. Mother always chose me last to get a spanking because she knew it would be a performance. She would laugh so hard she could not finish the job. My sister Maxine's job was to catch me before I made it under the house but she could never catch me. My brother William would run with me until he got a glimpse of the switch in Mother's hand, then he would fall back. I would stay under the house for hours, sometimes until dark or until someone would come out and tell me there was a snake under there. The screaming and crying would start all over again. However, when Dad got home he would come to get me and there would be no more screaming or crying because you just didn't do that with Dad. I crawled out from under that house and took my spanking like a big girl… yeah, right.

Mother loved to talk with all her cousins, especially Gerline, Sharing everything with her, because she was her cousin and friend. They lived in the same town. She often talked about Rossie and Rosy who had moved to California with their mother. How much she loved and missed all of them. When Lorene Flowers was born, a special star shined for her in the sky because God already knew she was a special child and she would soon come to be with him in heaven. She had such a graceful walk, so proud and assured like a princess.

Yes, a star was born when you were born, Mother. You are that star that seems so far but yet is so close and dear. Mother, I will always remember you. Your gentleness, your pride, and your struggle to survive with four children. And to live, even as you lay in your bed dying, not begging for your life or even thinking about yourself, but wanting to know, "Where is my baby Joyce? Is she ok? Where are my other children?" you asked. You will always be a part of me and I of you. I will never understand as long as I live why you were taken from us so early. I have felt your presence all of my life; you have been there in spirit. I feel your love and I know you feel my tears.

When my wonderful, beautiful mother was brutally murdered, I was seven, Maxine was nine and William five. Actually, we turned these ages after her death. I have been trying to write this book for over ten years. I knew I had to write it. Forty-eight years later it grieves me and saddens my spirit. I have to stop, pray, and cry because it's still so fresh in my mind. I will forever miss my mother.

The Story

It was a warm beautiful Sunday afternoon, Mother's Day, 1947. Dad had left home earlier and told my mother he would be back to take us to Grandmother Dellie's house for dinner. Mother dressed all of us for dinner and told my sister, brother, and me that we could go visiting for awhile. Mother was tired because she was pregnant with twins, so she and Baby Joyce, who was two-years old, decided to take a nap. The three of us went off to visit our friends.

We lived in the country where there were woods with many tall trees, and several roads leading to various places. Towns and general stores, woods and fields surrounded our house. William took one road to visit his friend Joe whose mother was Mrs. Cammie, a close friend of the family. Maxine and I took a different road to our friend's house about five miles away. Mother instructed us to be back in a couple of hours because Dad would be back and we would be leaving for dinner.

Approximately one or two hours later, we saw a new dark colored pick-up truck. It was driven by a man who I had never seen before and have never seen again. He drove up shouting, "If you girls want to see your mother alive, run home as fast as you can! There has been a terrible accident. I am going to look for your dad." Can you imagine? No, you can't unless you had been there. What was going through our young minds? An accident? Our mother? What was this man saying? Who is he?

Even now as I tell the story, my heart is racing, it is out of control. My sister and I started running, crying and praying as loud as we could, "God, please don't let our mother die." Running because the man had said that if we wanted to see her alive, we should run as fast as we could. We ran as fast as our little feet could go.

When we reached the house, the truck was there backed up to the porch. A mattress was on the bed of the truck and Dad was not there. Mother was lying there on her back moaning and groaning. The mattress was full of blood. We screamed and yelled, "Oh, my God, please help our mother. Don't let her die, please. Where is Joyce?" We started up the steps and someone said, "Don't go in there, girls. Joyce is dead."

Tears were rolling down our littlest faces. We were overwhelmed with sadness, hurt, anger, fear and confusion. We were so afraid, and where was our dad?

Mother was taken to a small hospital in Waldo, Arkansas. The doctors took one look and shook their heads saying that they were sorry, but they would not be able to help Mother. It was too serious and they did not have the equipment to help her. Mother was then taken to another hospital in Magnolia, Arkansas where she was admitted. Mother and Joyce's head had been slashed with an axe that Daddy used to cut wood for the fireplace and stove.

William was four years, eight months old. He turned five on August 31. We were told that William, his friend and friend's mother were coming to our house for wood and water from the well. When William heard mother moaning and groaning, he went inside to investigate. He stated that he had seen a short man jump off the back porch deck and run into the woods. "It looked like my dad," he said. The police were called and the hunt and search began. I can still hear the sound of those bloodhound dogs barking and sniffing everything and everyone. The dogs were searching for suspects all night. The police were asking questions and beating people to try to get information or a confession, even if it was a lie.

My brother, however, kept repeating that the man looked like my dad. The man had on the same hunting jacket that dad had worn on many occasions. I, too, remember that hunting jacket, red and black plaid with a hat to match. It must have been a popular set at the time because a lot of men bought them. They arrested a man named B. C., who was supposedly a friend of the family.

Dad always sent B.C. over to help mother by cutting wood and lighting the fireplace. He would also get water from the well for Mother and did different things around the house as a handyman. Mother treated B.C. like a friend and nothing more, drawing no attention to herself because Dad was extremely jealous. B.C. respected or feared him, and he loved Mother and her children. The day before Mother was attacked, Dad had B.C. over to sharpen the axe, but he didn't cut any wood that day. B.C. left the axe sticking into a block of wood and left.

My brother stuck with his story that the man was short and looked like Daddy. Dad kept telling my brother that the man was tall and looked like S. W. Dad considered S. W. as his rival and had accused him of having a crush on mother. I think Dad felt guilty because he was never home, always leaving her alone while he was out of town sometimes he was gone for months. After all, mother was young and beautiful and men were attracted to her. The police picked up S. W. and beat him continuously trying to make him confess. Finally they had to let him go because they believed him.

The investigation continued until B. C. was arrested. He stated that he had confessed, because they beat him so badly. He also stated that Daddy had paid him to kill mother, he did not kill Lorene and Joyce. B. C. went to prison for the murders, serving only seven years for four lives.

While Mother was in Magnolia Hospital, it was so sad and a little scary because she kept repeating, "No, Babe, no, Babe," moaning and groaning. Babe was Dad's nickname. Her head was all bandaged with gauze. She asked repeatedly, "Where is Joyce? Where is my baby?" And every time Dad went near her, she would bleed from the wound in her head saying, "No, no, Babe."

The police told the family that they were never to leave Dad alone with her because they strongly believed Dad did this to her, but they could not prove it yet.

Mother died approximately seven days after being admitted. The doctors said that she had asked about Joyce because she remembered that the baby was there when this tragedy happened and it was still on her subconscious mind. She never regained consciousness again. I feel so much pain about the loss of my mother, my sister Joyce, and the twins. They are gone forever. We will never see them again in this life.

The three of us have a steep mountain to climb. But what will be on the other side? We've got to climb it together. But, with love, dignity, pride and God on our side, we will make it.

Our journey started the day of the funeral. The funeral was the saddest I've ever seen. Poor Mama Carrie almost lost her mind. I don't remember seeing Dad at the funeral or the cemetery. He kept his distance. Later I saw him standing by his car. He did not come to the burial of Mother with the rest of the family, continuing to keep space between the two families.

Goodbye, my dear Mother. May you rest in peace. Mother, you never had a chance in life but you will never hurt or be hurt again. We were robbed of you at young ages and will miss you being there with us, With God's help and the love and support of our family, we will survive and make it through this. You will be in our hearts forever.

Chapter II

DADDY

Father of Approximately 18 Children

Dad was a bit older than Mother; more experienced, outgoing and seldom at home. I don't ever remember seeing him at dinner or bedtime with the family, or waking up seeing him in the morning; it was always Mother. There was always gossip floating around the little town of Waldo about our dad being quite a ladies' man, and that he was a womanizer. Perhaps it was the ladies pursuing him. My mother loved her husband regardless.

Dad drove people in his truck from city to city, sometimes to other states to work. I don't remember him sending money home. Always remembering my great grandparents Mollie, Dellie, Mama Carrie, and also Mother's sister Dorothy Faye supporting us. The rest of the family also did whatever they could to help.

There were times when Mother did not want to bother anyone, and I'm sure to protect Dad she didn't tell anyone that we had no shoes, clothes, or food. She was too ashamed, because the family was already very upset with Dad. In the winter, my sister and I would try to walk to school in the snow and rain. It was miles and miles to school. It was very cold and as we walked our feet would come out of the bottom of our shoes where we had put cardboard for soles trying to close up the holes. Our feet would be frozen. Thank God there was always a ram in the bush. Mama Carrie would send us a box of clothes including shoes and coats right on time. You know why? Because we serve an on-time God. We also ate at Mama Mollie's house often.

One year Dad left and was gone for approximately two years. He had

Left: Daddy

set up "housekeeping" with another family in Cleveland, Ohio. There was no contact with Mother at all. He didn't send her a penny but he expected her to wait faithfully and be there whenever he returned home. And guess what? She was. Maybe she waited out of fear, afraid not to wait. There were men who admired her but they were afraid to ask her out. Their parents were afraid for them to get involved with Mother, or even to talk to her. What power my dad had even when he wasn't even around. He was loved and respected by a lot of people in Waldo, both blacks and whites. He also did a lot of work for them; plumbing and working on their cars. But he put fear in a lot of people.

After Mother's death, he got remarried and he and his new wife raised ten children. We were not there. We were living in California with Grandma Carrie. We had very little communication with Dad. He called and wrote us maybe once a year. Mama never received any child support and he never came to visit, as if we didn't exist. Daddy did love us in his own way because he was always glad to hear from us when we called him, and when we went to visit him, he never wanted us to leave.

One year when we went to visit, Dad wanted to keep us with him. He had two children by his new wife, and he wanted us to stay with him, so he did not let us go back to California. Without any warning, he told our grandmother, "I'm keeping my children with me this time. They cannot go back with you." My grandmother almost died a second time. She was devastated. We begged and pleaded to go back home. We did not feel welcome at his home. We felt like strangers and not truly accepted by his new wife. Relatives on both side of the family pleaded and begged him to release us but Dad was adamant about us staying with him. His heart was hardened. So you know what we did? We couldn't take it and we ran away to California the first chance we got. Many people were on our side and wanted to see us go back to Mother's mom.

The next time I saw my dad I was an adult, and had two children. We were not about to go back to Arkansas even to visit. We were also afraid to stay there because he had never talked to us about who had killed Mother and being unsure about the truth made us uncomfortable.

One year when I went to visit Mother's grave, I took my two daughters, Pamela and Regina, with me. We visited my dad and he broke down and cried. Asking, "Why did you kids run away from me?" I felt terrible and sad for him. I did not know what to say because he was a stranger to me. I loved Dad.

Dad was a great gospel singer. He belonged to an awesome singing group and they were always called upon to perform at many church functions. Mother would be so proud, smiling and crying at the same time. Dad's mother, Mama Bertha, would shout for joy. Many years later as we got older and had families of our own, we started to communicate with our other sisters and brothers. I talked a lot with my sister Patsy. She and I took turns calling each other. She is also a great evangelist and I love to hear her pray. She and I did that quite often, interceding for the rest of the family. I love them all and I am sure they love us.

We heard various rumors about Dad and his heavy drinking, about him almost losing his mind, calling his children, by our names. We felt that those rumors were just that, rumors. We were young and doing our own thing so actually it just wasn't that important to us.

William always resented Dad because he never took time with him, he taught all of the other boys different trades (plumbing, cars, etc) but not him. My brother was in California and Dad was in Arkansas. My brother felt Dad should have taken him to Arkansas or come to California to spend some time with him. Dad got really sick and passed away in 1986. Prior to his passing, we were able to be with him and ask him the question, who killed our mother? And why? His reply was, "I don't know. I loved your mother." We were not convinced that he was telling the truth. Dad was dying and the truth of mother's death would be buried with him was difficult to accept.

Why Dad? Why couldn't you tell us the truth for once in your life and ease our wondering minds so you could die knowing you did the right thing. Goodbye to the dad I never knew. I pray you made peace with God, because you never did with the three of us.

Chapter III

MAMA CARRIE

Top Left: Mama Carrie (2)
Top Right:
Reggie and Connie Ridgeway
Second row:
Left: Mattie Davis (Family friend for
60 years)
Center: Aunt Connie
Right: Aunt Nellie
Bottom: Aunt Connie in her steward
uniform from church

Sisters
Left: Aunt Connie
Right: Mama Carrie

Top
Left: Willie Bussey
Right: Wife, Rosy Bussey

Bottom
Top left: Rossie group: her children, Connie, Jessie, Mandie
Top right: Her son, Kenny
Bottom left: Connie
Bottom right: Rozita and Michael

Grandmother Carrie got permission from Dad to take us to Santa Ana, California. What a job for Mama. Three children to raise and she had never even raised one. She left home at an early age giving guardianship to her mother to raise her daughter. She left Arkansas, to look for work, following her other sisters to California. She moved and found a job right away. Every month, she sent money home to her parents to help financially with her daughter.

Maxine, William, and I attended Roosevelt Elementary School, Willard Jr. High, and Santa Ana High School. Maxine continued her education at Santa Ana College and Orange Coast College in Costa Mesa, California, majoring in nursing. William, however, attended high school in Compton, California. He lived with relatives, the Bussey's, Rosy and her husband Willie. Everyone was so wonderful and understanding helping Mama in any and every way they could, having pity and much sadness for our family. Mom worked hard and saved enough money to take us on a vacation to see Dad and the rest of the family every summer. Mama Carrie was called Mama, Mrs. Carrie and GaGa. GaGa was her favorite name. She was called GaGa because her smart grandchildren could not say grandmother. Raising three small children was a huge task for her. Call it her cross or whatever you want.

Mama was an independent, God-fearing woman. She was an awesome woman who gave her all and then some. Mama was married to E. B. who had no knowledge of us coming back to live with them. Mama made the decision after the funeral. She was out of her mind with hurt and grief, but she felt this was the least she could do for her daughter. This was what Mother would have wanted.

Many people tried to understand her pain and grief. Her face was always so sad, but I never saw the tears she tried so hard to hide. We only saw her strength. I heard her crying and talking to God at night, asking Him why, why didn't you take me? Why my only child?

Mama's husband could not handle this imposition on his household. He felt rejected and jealous as if we had moved him completely out. Mama had put us first. He started drinking heavily, staying out late, playing around with other women and wanting to fight her. We put a stop to the fighting once and for all. No one was going to hurt another one of our loved ones if we could help it. One night we all gathered our little weapons, sticks, hammers and brooms and told him he had better not touch our grandmother. This was the last straw for him. E.B. gave Mama an ultimatum: "me or the grandkids." Mama told him to pack his clothes and get out. We didn't realize at the time what a decision she had made.

When we moved to the west side of Santa Ana, Mr. E.B. came with us because he was trying to work things out with Mama. We felt privileged that she had chosen us but E.B. only handled this situation for about one year. He soon met a widow named F. B., started an affair, and shortly after, moved in with her two blocks from where we lived. I was so sorry that she had lost the one man she truly loved for our sakes.

Mama's sister, Aunt Connie, was her right hand. She was also awesome; one of the strongest women I have ever known or met in my life. She was like the Godfather, only she was the Godmother of our entire family, a strong God-fearing woman. Her favorite sayings were always pray, treat people right, prayer is the answer to every situation, there is good in everybody, let God handle and work the problem out. Mama always lived close to Aunt Connie. It was God and Aunt Connie that helped Mama keep her sanity. And, of course, the three of us gave her reasons to keep going.

We loved Aunt Connie, she was one of the stewardesses who sat in the front row of our church, Johnson Chapel A.M.E. in Santa Ana, California. She wore all white except for a little black hat. She really enjoyed the church services and loved to hear the choir sing. She was always smiling and hugging everyone. Whenever I was going to lead a song or sing a solo I would go to the microphone, pick it up, and look at my aunt for support because I knew the Holy Spirit dwelled in her. Before I could finish the first verse, that left leg would go up into the air and she would let out a scream that touched my soul and made my hair stand up. I was inspired and encouraged. I would see the tears rolling down her cheeks and knew that she was remembering and reliving what had happened to Mother.

Many people from all sections of Orange County would come to Aunt Connie to make those famous cakes, tea-cakes, and pies. Some just wanted to eat some of her meals, she was a wonderful cook. She gave wanted advice to the young and encouraged the old. Aunt Connie put God first in everything she did and one of her favorite songs was "What A Friend We Have In Jesus," and "Precious Lord." My aunt had two daughters Rossie and Rosy. They were her pride and joy. These children were from her first marriage and she meant the world to them.

Aunt Connie talked to Mama every day. And would always cook a little too much on purpose, and would bring the leftovers to our house and play it off by saying, "Here, Carrie, I cooked too much again tonight." We always had a nice house with beautiful clothes and plenty to eat. With all these things, however, there was still a deep void in our lives because we missed our mother. Everyone looked at us with such sympathy and pity not really knowing what to say. It seemed as if they wanted to cry or just hold us in their arms. At church, visiting the neighbors, everyone knew the horrible story about that dreadful day.

Mama kept us very active in church. Sunday School, and choir rehearsals were our outings. We also had to attend Bible League on Sunday evening. Maxine was always the elected Sunday School delegate for the annual conference. She was also the secretary and taught a class to the little ones. I loved Sunday School. I would give the report at the closing of Sunday School. I also loved to go to the conference because it was very interesting to me. We were allowed to walk to the movies with our friends and, as we got older, to chaperoned parties at the recreation center with Mrs. Mattie Davis, Mrs. Mattie Lang, Mrs. E. R. and Mrs. J. H.

I believe one of my callings in life was singing. How I loved to sing. As a youngster I would play church or a nightclub singer. I would use the broom as my mic and sing in the backyard all afternoon. Maxine loved to play nurse; she was good at it too. Not only would she play nurse. She would actually help the neighbors. That was, and still is, her calling.

William was the youngest of us and found joy in playing. He loved to play cowboys and Indians, and Batman and Robin with his friends. I believe he wanted to tire himself out so he could sleep at night, trying to forget what he had seen. Everyone was very compassionate to us, especially to William giving him gifts, love and plenty of attention. However, they did not realize how much we were hurting inside and needed help. We needed to talk about how we were robbed, how much we missed our mother. No one talked to us about what had happened. No one came to our rescue. We definitely needed professional help. But in 1947, no one thought to seek professional help for three small black children.

The teachers and principal at Roosevelt Elementary were wonderful and understanding. I am remembering when Mama took us there to register us, she had to go into the office and talk with Mrs. Green, the principal, and tell her what had happen to our mother. The principal hugged Mama and they both broke down and cried. The principal expressed her sympathy to her.

Mama Carrie was wonderful, making sure we had wholesome lunches and that we were always neat and clean. Cleaning houses for a living (was the only work she could find) for wealthy school teachers and doctors. They were very good to her and knew what had happened to her daughter. They always gave her a little extra something. I resented her cleaning houses, always feeling that they didn't appreciate all those little extra personal things she did for each and every one of them.

Mama was always so serious and tired, never smiling or laughing a lot. When I attended Roosevelt, I was a very slow learner. I had a problem retaining information and I would daydream all through class pretending Mother was alive and imagining what she would say when I got home from school. Things like how was school, what did you learn today, smiling and listening all at the same time. I just couldn't get it together, couldn't catch on. My mind kept drifting back to that horrible day. The teacher would call on me and I honestly wouldn't know the answer. I didn't even know what she was talking about. I had not been paying attention. I was always so confused because I couldn't think fast enough like the other kids. Thank God for Mrs. Gant. She was stern, tough and a very callous teacher. She took time with me, she was very patient and compassionate. Our birthdays were on the same day. I'll never forget her and all the extra time she took with me because slowly I began to progress. I stopped daydreaming and began to concentrate on my assignments.

One of the activities at school was square and folk dancing. I never had a partner because none of the boys wanted to take my hand and dance with me. Let's face it, this was in the forties and there were only four or five blacks in the whole school. I would pretend it didn't bother me day after day, pretending it was o.k. I was seven years old, of course it bothered me and I didn't understand. I would silently cry because it broke my heart to be rejected like I was an animal or from another planet. I didn't mention it to my grandmother because I thought she would come up to the school and cause problems so I kept it to myself.

One day one of the girls, Nan, left her dance partner, came and took my hand and started to dance with me. That broke the race barrier in my class. The next day one of the guys came and said, "Come on, Dorothy, be my partner." He looked around and said, "I'll beat up anyone that laughs." He was one of the most popular guys in the whole school.

I will never forget D. T. In baseball he always chose me to be on his team. The rest saw that I was a good player and wanted me also but I always went with D. T. This young man made a difference in my life and didn't even know it. D. T. told me not to pay any attention to those other kids because they were just dumb. "You can't help it if your skin is another color, and you're better in sports and can sing better than any of them." From that day on I started to feel good about myself and believe in who I was, a special child of God.

My brother was even slower than I. He really needed help. At an early age he would cut class and play at anyone's house all day to keep from going to school. Mama had a problem, but she didn't realize how serious the problem was with my brother. Maxine was affected more than either of us. She was the oldest and was closer to mother. She had seen and heard more than William and I. She had been at home most of the time and she and mother had talked a lot. However, in school my sister was the one that excelled faster. I was always proud of her. I always thought to myself, "My sister is so smart. She knows everything."

While living on the east side of Santa Ana, we met a family by the name of Meals. Mama and Mrs. Meal became close friends and we were friends with her children. Her sons C. N. and O. N. were a little bit older than we were. Tine and Betsy were more our age. We walked to church together on Sundays. We did everything together. Mom and Mrs. Meal would potluck many weekends after church. The Meal family were not church going people until they met us. Our family was so excited about going to church, they got interested and wanted that excitement too. The girls joined the choir and even Mrs. Meal joined the adult choir with Mama.

Mama really needed this. Mrs. Meal's oldest son C. N. was very popular. He played football in high school and college. We were like one big happy family. When we moved to second street on the west side, we continued to go to church and be friends with the Meals. We also met many new friends. The Jones girls, Earlene, Mattie, and many more. Moving near Aunt Connie helped when we had a problem expressing ourselves or felt Mama didn't understand. We would go to her and she always had the perfect solution.

Mama's other sister that lived in California was Aunt Nellie. Aunt Nellie was out-going and jazzy. She traveled a lot but lived in Los Angeles. I admired and loved her. Sometimes the three of us would spend summer vacation in Los Angeles. If Aunt Nellie was in town, I would stay with her for a week or until I got on her nerves. We would also visit with our favorite cousins. Some were much younger but we had fun visiting for the summer.

We visited Rosy and Rossie, Aunt Connie's daughters. Rosy would let us take turns staying with her and Willie. Sometimes Maxine and I would go at the same time. She and her husband were a lot of fun. They were young and loved to do fun things. A lot of the young people in Compton loved to go to their home, having a lot of respect for them and their home. They had no children of their own, so all of us were their adopted children. We loved to watch them dance to the blues and oldies-but-goodies. Boy, was that fun.

Then there was sweet loving Cousin Rossie. She had six children and was married to a very strict and controlling husband. We didn't spend too much time over at her house, but I didn't care how strict, he was loving and kind to me. I loved her and her children and would stay overnight, the weekend, or sometimes a week. Rossie told me that she and our mother were not only first cousins but best friends, as close as any sister could be. She always told us how good and kind mother was and that she understood why we did not spend as much time with her, but her children were like our own little sisters and brothers. As years passed, we started calling Rossie and Rosy Aunt Rossie and Auntie as if they were mother's sister's. They said mother would approve of our decision. I spent more time over at their house than Maxine or William. I even called her children's grandmother Mama Maude their father's mother. Rossie and her husband Jessie separated and later divorced in 1959. They had been married for sixteen years. Three years later, she enrolled in Henrietta's Beauty College in 1962 for sixteen months. She declared that these were the best times of her life, and she had made many new friends. After graduating from the beauty college, Rossie opened her own beauty shop on Broadway Street in Los Angeles.

When we went to L.A. for the summer, this gave our grandmother a much needed break. Plus, it gave her time to regroup. In the sixties, Mama had been corresponding with a childhood sweetheart in Arkansas by the name of Mr. Fletcher. He eventually asked her to marry him. His wife had died, and he was lonely. Mama was excited and delighted asking us how we felt about it. We told her to go for it. She also discussed this with her mom and the rest of the family. Everyone agreed that she should accept and be happy. "Say yes. All of your children are grown and have moved out."

Mama called Mr. Washington and accepted his proposal. He then began to make all of the arrangements to move her back to Arkansas.

We were sad because Mama was leaving but very happy for her because for once since her child died she could be happy again. They were very happy and went to church together. Both seniors worked in the garden, breathed fresh air, and had a beautiful home. We were a little nervous for Mama because Daddy lived in the same town and there was never any closure on Mother's death. But she was a brave woman and had many family members living there. This was her chance to be happy again. Mama had done a wonderful job raising her daughter's three children. She was satisfied and knew Aunt Connie was there for us very close by.

Mama's husband died some years later and we went back for the funeral. She continued to stay in Arkansas because she had made many friends, was active in church, and was reestablished. She continued to come to California to visit us every summer.

The summer of 1983 Aunt Connie went to Arkansas and while visiting Mama, she noticed that she did not look well. She had lost a lot of weight and was trying to hide the fact that she did not feel well and was always tired. Aunt Connie returned home and suggested we go to Arkansas and bring Mama to California because something was seriously wrong with her sister. Mama said she did not want to tell us that she was sick because we already had so much on us with Dad being sick and having cancer. But we quickly explained to her that she had always been there for us and that she came first after God.

We rented a U-Haul truck, packed up all of her belongings and brought her back to California. We made an appointment with a local doctor and was told that Mama had colon cancer. This broke our hearts. She was already being treated for high blood pressure by the doctors in Arkansas. We were also told that if they operated on her, there was a strong possibility that she would die because she was so weak, and her blood pressure was too high. We decided to listen to her Dr. and wait until he decided it was okay.

After surgery, Mama stayed with Maxine. She had a colostomy and was very sad about this. But she was alive. She had never been sick in her life only a few minor colds. She had never even been in a hospital. We were all devastated. Mama started losing weight and never accepted the fact that she had to keep her weight down and eat certain foods. She kept saying, "I look awful." In the south, the bigger you were the healthier they thought you were. If you were too thin, you were poorly.

Maxine was the first one to take care of Mama. She was excellent with her and the only one that had nursing skills. And brother William was married to Trina and worked every day. It would not have been fair for him to take her to his house. I was separated from my husband and was living in Inglewood with my cousin Connie. Mama was recovering well and I would go see her every weekend and do what I could to help my sister. Mama wanted to come live with me and give Maxine a break. I felt badly about not being able to have her stay with me so I went back to my husband and took my grandmother with me.

Mama lived with me until she passed away. She became very ill and was getting worse each day, my neighbors were wonderful. Connie Ridgeway especially. She looked in on her while I was at work, coming daily. And made sure she ate her lunch delivered by meals-on-wheels. Mama complained about the food not tasting good but I knew it wasn't the food, it was her. The medicine made the food taste different causing her to lose her appetite. Another dear neighbor, Mattie Smith, gave me encouragement and much needed prayers. Mom continued to lose weight and complained that her skin was hanging. "Look, I don't even look normal," she would say.

Before this tragedy happened to mother, Mama was a very attractive woman and very proud. But when her daughter died, she died with her. She blamed herself for Mother's death because Mother went to visit her one year and did not want to return to Arkansas to her husband but she was pregnant. So Mama thought she was giving her the best advice a mother could give by telling her to go home, have her babies, and try to work things out with her husband. Mama wrote her a letter stating if things remained the same and it did not work out, she would send for her and all her children to come back to California to live. But Dad had intercepted the letter and Mama never saw her child alive again.

Mama died December 1987. That was a sad Christmas for our family. We returned all the gifts we had bought for her. Again, overwhelmed and devastated, we tried to go on. We struggled so hard to get our lives back together after losing our precious grandmother, our rock, our friend. The strong grandmother who gave her whole life for three grandchildren, her teachings and spirit will be with us forever. Rest in peace, Precious Gem. We will continue to be ever so grateful for all that you gave, you gave your all. We feel your presence daily.

At Mama's grave the day of the funeral, I heard Aunt Connie say to her sister, "Goodbye, my sister, I will see you soon." She said this not knowing she would be the next to die. In 1988, another unexpected tragedy occurred in our lives. I was at work in Los Angeles, California. March 29, 1988 when I received a call from one of our close family friends, Mrs. Mattie Davis, and my sister-in-law Trina. They were calling to tell me that Aunt Connie had been shot. That was the worst call I had received in 41 years. Crying and screaming, I ran to my car to leave for Orange County. Aunt Connie's granddaughter Maudie also worked for the Los Angeles Unified School District. She called me from another department and asked me what had happened? She wanted to know if her grandmother was dead or alive. I told her I didn't know but was leaving for Santa Ana and would meet her there. I was worried and wanted to know exactly what had happened. Was she dead? Oh, God, not my precious Aunt Connie. I kept saying this over and over. I was driving on the freeway as fast as my car could go, praying to be stopped by the police so that they could escort me. Never saw not one. Everyone drove as fast as they could to get to Aunt Connie's house. Family, friends, everybody was there. I drove alone arriving only to find out that she had died. I started screaming as loud as I could. She had been shot and killed supposedly by her ninety-plus-year-old husband. That tore my heart to pieces. Everybody was saddened and shocked. All who knew and didn't know her, were angry, confused and hurt. I was going out of my mind.

Aunt Connie had been married to her husband for forty-seven years. Everyone called him Uncle Ted. My aunt was killed exactly 41 years after my mother's tragic death. We can only wonder and ask ourselves why. What happened? Why my mother? Why Aunt Connie? Was there some sort of a curse on our family or was it just circumstantial? Two beautiful people that loved life and people so much, who didn't bother anyone.

Aunt Connie's death touched so many people. People in and out of her church. Her children almost lost their minds. She was 88 years old and wasn't even sick. She loved her husband, and was always there for him. One of the members from the church, Mrs. Mattie Lang, said that the night before her death Aunt Connie was asked to pray the closing prayer. She prayed a powerful prayer that would make your hair stand up and in her prayer she was asking God to take care of her husband and to bless him. There was not a dry eye in the whole church after she finished. She loved everyone, and above all, she loved life.

Aunt Connie was godmother, not only to our family, but to many. Everyone that met or knew her loved her. My aunt's funeral was the largest funeral that has ever been held in the black community. There were reporters covering her death from the Orange County Register and various other papers. They asked questions, got statements, just really tried to figure out what had happened, why would this old man kill his wife of forty-seven years like a dog, an animal in the streets.

I had never seen her not going to church. Every Sunday she was there. She worked in the church. She was a stewardess and one of the mothers in the church. Aunt Connie is missed by all. Always cooking for people, inviting them over for dinner after church. Just being there for everybody with advice, love, and a big hug and a kiss. Jesus was her friend even until the end. What a friend I had in my dear sweet Aunt Connie, my guiding angel.

Chapter IV

MAXINE, MY SISTER, MY FRIEND

Psalm 23: "The Lord is My Shepherd"

Top Group: Maxine Bottom Group Left top: her daughter Vickie
Bottom left: Licia (daughter) Bottom right: Rickie (son) (2)Love47

Maxine's grandchildren

Top left (group): Lil Rickie, Dad Rickie, Kim Rick's daughter. Rickie's children: Kimberly, Ricquida, Richard

My sister was totally devastated over Mother's death. She, being the oldest child. Maxine told me she had blocked out a lot of things that had happened in our home when Mother was alive. The more we talked about Dad and mother, the more she started to remember things that had happened years ago.

Maxine was quiet and on the shy side when we were kids. Very observant of everything. I got on her nerves a lot I am sure because I was loud, talked a lot, was always joking and making people laugh. I loved to see people laugh. If they were laughing, I thought they were happy and this made me happy. So this was my specialty. I could imitate anyone. She would laugh sometimes, but at other times I think I embarrassed her. She has never gotten over Mother and Joyce being killed. Oh, how I feel the pain for my sister.

When we were growing up, I always watched my sister, so very sad and lonely; always sitting alone, just staring into space as if she was looking for Mother to walk into the room at any given second. Sometimes tears would be rolling down her face. We were confused and bitter. We have been friends and sisters, and sure we had our arguments and make up times, but never anything serious. I love my sister. Mama Carrie always dressed us alike. However, as we got older, we told her that enough was enough. We didn't like the same clothes or the same colors. She always had us in blue and pink.

We also discovered we had different friends. My sister was very popular with all the males. She had a lot of male friends. Yes, female too. But she said it was easier to get along with the guys. She was very popular with the Mexican-Americans, male and female. At that time, the blacks and Mexicans stuck together. We partied, were in a car club together, ate and slept at each others' houses. Maxine dressed like the Chicanos and combed her hair teased up high like her female friends. Unlike me, I did not have the hair for the high tease, but sometimes I would wear the jeans and flannel shirt that we thought were tough, and that was a very popular style in the fifties and sixties.

Maxine was very popular in school and an A-student. She graduated and went to college for a year. Maxine had many marriage proposals. Buck even gave her a ring before he went away to the Air Force. She really did not want to marry him but Mama and Aunt Connie were hoping she would since both families went to the same church. They told her he was a fine man. Maxine finally told them, "I am not marrying him, I don't love him." They were so disappointed but it was her life and they had to respect her opinion. Several other guys also pursued her but her response was always, "No, no, no. Let's just be friends."

Maxine worked part time while in junior high school and all her jobs were helping elderly ladies in their homes. She did everything for them. I always admired my sister for this because I was totally the opposite. I would always ask her how she could do this kind of work and her reply was, "There's nothing to it. I love taking care of and helping the elderly and sick people." I told her that she was so good at it that she was a blessing to those people. I was more the customer service type person, taking care of the business at hand.

Maxine has three beautiful children that I am very close to: Vickie, Rickie and Licia. I love them so much. She also has four grandchildren and I am their special auntie. What an honor!

In 1969 I moved to Los Angeles, California and didn't see my sister very much. However, one year I persuaded her to move to Los Angeles. Reluctantly, she said ok and I was a very happy sister. I got busy looking for an apartment for her. In the meantime, she and the kids moved in with us. She came but never adjusted to Los Angeles and eventually moved back to Orange County in 1977. I've always had a special love, concern, and sense of protection for my sister because she is my best friend. I've always wanted her to have the best, to have everything I had and more. I have always tried to show her how much I loved her. I will always be there for her. This poem was written for me by Maxine for my birthday on April 26, 1997. I will forever cherish this card. To My Loving Sister on Her Birthday:

Dear Sister, You're the one everyone leans on, you're the one everyone looks up to. You're the little soldier who is the leader of the band. You're the mountain everyone wishes to climb. You're the beautiful little stream that runs through the valley of love. You're the beautiful little flower that grows in the garden for everyone to see.

There is only the three of us and we all love each other. Only the three of us know what we have lived and no one needs to know the past. We have lived, loved, laughed and cried together. Life is not promised to us tomorrow, so live your life to the fullest. No more being the little soldier, no more being the little stream. Let everyone climb their own mountain and take their own bruises. You stay happy. I wish you love and happiness. May all your dreams come to pass. God bless you and I wish you a Happy Birthday with all my love, forever, Your Sis, Maxine.

I love you, my sister Maxine. I'm so sorry we were robbed of our mother at such a young age but our lives were spared for a reason. We've come a long way by the grace of God and God has used your talents to help and give love to many weak and helpless people. We will continue to be there for each other for the rest of our lives. It's okay to lean on me, Sis, when you're not strong. I'll be your strength and I'll help you carry on forever.

Chapter V

WILLIAM, MY LITTLE BROTHER, MY FRIEND

William's Children

Left: William
Right: Trina
Lower: Williams Children
David, Dwayne, Vincent, Rachelle [Center: Dwayne; Right: Donny & Rachelle (getting married)]
Bottom: Left: Vincent, David (pee wee); Center: Vincent (Graduation), Bottom: David and Pilar (getting married); Left Bottom: David

William's grandchildren
Top: Wm, Candice, Vincent (Vincent's daughter); Nakisha (David's
daughter), Ashley (Rachelle's Daughter); Candice; Lil David, Jennifer
(David's kids); Lil Donny (Rachelle's son)

Bottom left: Joe McDade and William; Middle: Sims, Johnny, Allen, Joe, Noland, Willie
Carroll, Willie, William, Jimmy, Gloria, Mr. and Mrs. Duffey, Earl. Right Top: Sally and
Earl. Greg's graduation, Gloria.

My brother William was four years, nine months old when our mother was murdered. He had been at a neighbor's house playing and Cammie mother's friend decided to go visit Mother for a little while, also to get wood and water. That was when the nightmare began. William ran up the steps first just to say hello but heard the moaning and walked into a horrible scene, finding Mother and Joyce laying in pools of blood. He was terrified and afraid. The grass and wild flowers were very tall so he couldn't get a good look at the perpetrator running from the scene. William said he didn't know who to help first, his mother or his baby sister so he ran outside to get Cammie. She came running inside to see why he was so frantic and saw the two bodies. Cammie went running, screaming and crying to the closest neighbor to get help because we did not have a telephone.

Word of mouth spread to everyone and the town was in shock. Relatives, friends, everyone was horrified and outraged. Then started the questions, beatings, bloodhound dogs and arrests. The police were at our house until late at night with Dad, William, my sister, me, including many others. The police continued asking my brother questions about what he remembered about the man he saw running from the house. My brother kept telling the police he was like my dad. "Dad, it looked like you. He had on a jacket like yours and was little like you." Dad said, "No, Son, you told me he was tall." William was so confused. Imagine how confusing this was to a four-year-old.

The police finally took William to a different area of the yard away from Dad to question him. William was very tired and sleepy. The police beat so many people that night trying to make someone tell something, or just to confess to the double homicide, everyone was tired and hungry. Finally they beat this man so badly that he confessed to the murders. He was short and owned a black, red and white jacket. B.C. confessed, stating that had Dad paid him to do it, and then later he stated that he did not do it. I believe the police would have beaten him to death.

They found bloody clothes at his house which he swore had been planted there. He had an alibi and could verify that he was home all evening. The police had to book someone for these brutal murders so B.C. was sent to prison still denying everthing.

Then there was the funeral. So sad, so many people from everywhere came to pay respects to Mother and Joyce for the last time. But the baby had already been buried. Who could have done such a terrible thing? Of course everyone had their own opinion. I was so glad when the funeral was over. People were falling out all over the church and I felt afraid, sad and depressed. I knew I would never see my mother again.

Every place we went it seemed that people knew the story. We could hear them whispering, "Those poor little children. Their mother and two-year-old sister were brutally murdered. What a shame."

William slept with the light on and his head was always under the covers. He always kept a weapon under the mattress and had awful nightmares. He had a best friend with whom he played cowboys and Indians daily. One afternoon his friend accidentally hung himself in his closet. William was the one to find him and could not get him down so he held onto him for hours until help came. Another tragic event that he witnessed, devastating him once again.

William was very protective of my sister and me. He is one of the sweetest and most sincere brothers any sister could ask for. He is my little brother, my best friend. Anytime I call him for anything he is there for me. Maxine and I are very protective of him also. We didn't allow anyone to hurt his feelings or get out of line with him in anyway.

Rosy's husband told Mama he was going to teach William how to work in their business, a cleaning service. William met Trina Duffey, a neighbor who lived across the street from the Bussey's. They started dating and soon got married. They were both still very young. Trina's family was wonderful and fun. They were a Christian family and Mr. Duffey loved to play baseball and volleyball with us. We loved to see the Duffey's do the jitterbug. Mrs. Duffey was always cooking something good to eat and she loved to entertain. Trina had a younger sister named Gloria who was always doing her own thing with her set of young friends.

One year there was a surprise in the Duffey household. Little Earl was born. What a joy! He was so handsome and loved by all. William and Trina started their family at a young age. He went to the Army, but only for a short time because they had three children and his wife needed him home. He got an honorable discharge and came home. Trina and Willie bought a home in Santa Ana. They were one of the youngest couples to buy a home. They have three very handsome sons: Dwayne, David, Vincent; and a beautiful daughter, Rachelle. I love them very much and they love and respect me. This makes me a special aunt once again.

My brother was always a sharp dresser, the life of the party, loved by males and females. His nickname was Bandit. His wife and I were like sisters, not sisters-in-law. We were always together. I've always had so much compassion and sympathy for my brother, even now that we are adults. I feel the pain and hurt that he has had to endure and want to continue to protect him. By doing extra things for him so he can be happy, I did not realize that I was crippling him more and more. Then there were times that I wanted to shake him and ask him to think, think about what he saw that day and who he saw running away from the house.

I married for the third time and wanted my brother to give me away but he was totally against it. He told me he felt bad vibes, and so did I, but I went on with the wedding. He asked me, "Do you have to marry everyone you date?" I laughed but then really started to think about what he was asking. I told my brother that from now on I would let God send me my next husband. "Amen," he said. He was so pleased to hear this.

My brother is loved and respected by all his nieces and nephews. They think he is so cool. He is the uncle everyone wants: handsome and a lot of fun. Now he is the proud grandfather of eight. Be happy, my little brother. One day God will give you the courage and strength to reveal who you saw looking back at you in those fields and it will free your mind. It is an honor to have a brother like you.

Chapter VI

ME, MYSELF, AND I

Psalm 40:

"I Waited Patiently for the Lord."

My years at Santa Ana High School were fun and exciting. After being a Brownie and Girl Scout at Roosevelt Elementary and a cheerleader at Willard Junior High, I was now in the big leagues. I was good in sports and had lots of friends of all races. But the fondest memory of all was being a part of the singing group, The Debonets. Dorothy Jones, Earlene Herron, Doris Lewis, my sister Maxine and myself made up this awesome and popular group. We could have and should have made it very big in the music business. Another friend was the manager who wrote and played for the group. We went to her house to rehearse once a week. Awesome at writing original songs and playing songs by various artists. We sounded identical to the original groups and we were in demand.

The Debonets sang at a dance at the Disneyland Hotel for the Black Barbers Association of Orange County and at a school assembly with the Brothers at Santa Ana High School. We also sang at beach parties, the Harmony Ballroom in El Monte, and were on the Al Jarvis and Ed Sullivan Show. We were willing to sing for any and all occasions. After having had all of these wonderfully positive experiences, I did something stupid. I got pregnant. I was devastated and so was the group. I was angry with myself, wondering how I could have been so careless! I had everything going for me! Mrs. J.H., my godmother, wanted me to go to college. She told my grandmother that she would send me to college, pay for everything, since she had no children of her own although she did have stepchildren. My schooling and the Debonets had to be put on hold for a long time. I could see the disappointment in Mama and Mrs. J.H. I had disappointed them, my family and friends. But because they were family and friends, they were very supportive and saw me through my pregnancy. And the merry-go-round begins.

Top: My son, Greg, and me Greg is escorting me into Church. I did a concert.
Middle: me and my daughter, Debbie. Concert. Top Singing group Debonet
Left to right: Me, Maxine, Dorothy Jones, Doris Lewis Spencer, Earlene Herron

Top left: Group (Easter): Mattie, Me, Barbara, Johnny, Maxine, Sally. Seated: Gladys

Top right: Pam, Barbara Ann (their aunt), Sims, Debbie

Left: Thelma Small. Mother in law: my girl's grandmother

Middle: Patsy, her mother Jessie, Johnny (funeral)

Right: Jessie, Johnny, Me (funeral)

Left: Mother's Day
Marla's: Pam, Debbie, Regina, Standing: me
Middle: Greg and Me
Right: Greg, me, Regina (Thanksgiving at Jessie's cuz)

Bottom left:
Debbie and me (Graduation Curtis Jr., Carson Jr. High).
Center: Jean Reeves Pitts
Right:
Me, Wm, Maxine

In loving memory of

Edgar r:Nathaniel Spencer, Jr.

October 31 , 1934 -:- August 10, 1992

Top left: jr

Center: Jr's brothers Wilbert and Jr.

Right: Me and Jr.

Jr; Harvey (Betty's husband) & Betty (cousin); me & Jr.

Left: Betty Harvey (sis), Betty;s mother

HUSBAND #1

I met my first husband when he arrived from Boise, Idaho in the fifties. He came to California to live with his Uncle Bill. He was tall, fair, had black curly hair, and was always smiling. He was very handsome. He was a new guy in town so you know the news spread like wildfire. And being in a small town with very few blacks, of course, all the teenagers and young adults had to go meet this new guy in town. His uncle was known and liked by everyone so it was easy to go over to his house (but we didn't dare). Party, yes, we had to plan a big party and invite him.

But guess what uncle Bill wanted to have, a get acquainted party for his nephew at his home. He got in touch with several of us to plan it and we invited everyone. There was a one-hundred percent turn out.

He was almost six years older than I, but he asked me to be his girl. At Mama's and Uncle Bill's request, he and I were married in Kingman, Arizona because I was pregnant. They said it was the right thing to do. Mama was so sad because she felt that I was just a baby having a baby. I felt terrible because this is not what my grandmother wanted for me. She wanted all of us to go to college, get our education, be lawyers, doctors, school teachers, but not mothers at sixteen. "I've let you down, Mama. I am so very sorry." She assured me it was okay. Once again my wonderful Aunt Connie was there to encourage Mama, to let her know she was there for her. She knew how disappointed she was because all parents want the best for their children, but she is not the first and wouldn't be the last to make a mistake, stated Aunt Connie.

Ashamed, but I never stopped going to church. And when Pamela was born I took my child with me. My friends helped to take care of her. They

came over and got her dressed for church. Many people said this is not the end of the world Dorothy. It happens all the time.

I continued to go to night school for a little while, but had to drop out because, guess what? I was pregnant again with Regina, ten and one-half months later. On December 28, 1957, my second child was born, another girl. So I thought well, okay what now? The group continued to sing for a little while without me. I was the lead singer but others could also lead. They were getting married and starting families of their own. My children's father and I drifted apart but I continued to have the support of both our families and all my friends.

His Uncle Bill was so wonderful to my children and me. We will never forget him. And he was married to a wonderful, special person named Jessie. She was so sweet and kind and especially supportive of me. She was always wanting to know if there was anything she could do, if we needed anything. She was always so cool and calm, letting no one upset her, always smiling and cheerful. I wished everyone was like Aunt Jessie. They had a special daughter named Patsy, Pat for short. She and my daughters were inseparable. My husband had two brothers, Jeffrey and Andrew, who I loved. I did not consider them my brothers-in-law, they were my brothers.

My husband also had two sisters Carolyn and Barbara. Carolyn and I were very close in age. I loved her and we were so much alike. I was only one year older than her. I always had a lot of compassion for her because I felt the family was too strict with her. She was an A-student, never missed any school, but always had so many chores to do at home, having no time for fun or herself. Sometimes I would help her so she would finish faster and do something else like have some fun, but the whole family kept a close eye on Carolyn. I would often say that they treated her like Cinderella and

I hated this. She explained that she had made a little mistake in Idaho and the family would never let her forget it. She was sent to California so her grandmother, could keep an eye on her. She also had three overprotective brothers. Carolyn and all of her brothers arrived before their mother, step- father, and sister Barbara Ann who was really pretty and spoiled. Grandma was in charge until her daughter, Thelma, arrived. The mother had already bought her home through Uncle Bill so all they had to do was move in when she arrived.

My husband's mother and I had our differences for a while but we eventually grew mentally and spiritually over the years. Neither my husband nor I worked on our marriage like we should have. We didn't keep people out of our personal business; his family or mine, his friends or mine. His mother had a big influence on him and I hated this. James, his step-dad, tried to tell her many times to stay out of our marriage and let us work things out for ourselves (he was totally cool and stayed neutral). I was taught to respect my elders so I tried hard to listen and respect his mother.

My children's father was gone for six years. Waiting for him to return was devastating for us. I was a young woman. When he returned, he was mean, bitter, and extremely jealous. We had definitely grown apart. My patience was running out. The night he came home, I was down the street from where I lived, playing cards with friends. I didn't go there often, but this particular night I got my babysitter Meme to come over so I could go, not knowing my husband would be home that night. What a shock I was in for when he showed up at my friend's house.

I was smoking a cigarette, even though I didn't smoke. He approached me and knocked it out of my hand (mistake). Everyone was in disbelief. Mainly because they were surprised to see him there. His brother Andrew was very upset to see him knock the cigarette out of my hand. He tried to speak to his older brother. He was glad to see him but did not like what he did. Andrew shook his head and walked off. Everyone else was wide-eyed and open-mouthed, some of the ladies were in tears suspecting what I was probably going to endure for the rest of the evening.

My husband was in a terrible mood and asked where the children were. I answered that they were at home with the babysitter. He stated that he didn't want his kids staying with no babysitter. "How often do you have a sitter?" He took me back to the apartment and started asking all kinds of questions, searching drawers and looking in closets. I was really nervous and my babysitter was frightened by him. "I won't leave you tonight. I will go home in the morning." She stayed in the room with the girls where they were already asleep. Right away he wanted to go to bed and I got sick to my stomach. I made all kinds of excuses, but he didn't buy not one of them, he would not hear of it. He made love as if he was angry with the whole world. Right then I knew that I didn't want this or him anymore; it was over.

The next morning I got up and my husband had a handkerchief with the initial J on it. He wanted to know to whom it belonged. I stated that I didn't know. He then asked me about Junior Spencer (we called him Jr.). Someone had told him that I had been dating Junior Spencer. "This is why you didn't want to go to bed with me. You want him." At this point, my babysitter left reluctantly and told me that I should call her if I needed to. "I don't like him at all and I am scared for you and the girls. Please be careful."

Things started to escalate and my husband called one of his friends nicknamed Boris to come over. His grandmother A.J. came over and saw that things were getting out of hand. She called for her son Bill to come home from work. He told me to get on the phone and call Jr. so we could get this cleared up. I called Jr., told him what was going on and warned him that he had called his friend Boris to come over. He said he would be right over, he was not afraid of neither one of them. But he did play it safe and brought his friend Milton with him. I could see they both had weapons.

My husband asked Jr. if he was going out with me. Jr. said what did she say? He replied that I had said no. He then told Jr. that if he wanted me he could have me. Jr. said, "Your wife is a beautiful and a respectable woman with a lot of class. Any man would be a fool not to want such a fine woman, so I'm saying you are a damn fool. But if you don't want her, I'll take her and your kids and you better not lay a finger on her after I leave. If you want to kick someone's ass, kick mine."

About this time Uncle Bill walked in asking what the hell was going on. He asked Jr., Milton, and Boris to leave. He could do this since the apartment building belonged to him. He then asked my husband, "What in the hell is wrong with you?" He said Jr was going out with my wife and I found one of his handkerchiefs in the drawer. Uncle Bill said, "Don't be a fool. You've been gone six years and your wife and kids are here with you now. Dorothy is a beautiful young woman and I don't know anything about her going with Jr. I'd like to know who told you this crap." Uncle Bill told my husband you and your family can stay in this apartment cheap, get a job and stop worrying about all the past bullshit.

After everyone had gone, he continued to interrogate me about things that I had been doing. He was really getting on my very bad side and making me nervous. The girls were afraid of him and very nervous about all that had gone on that morning. We didn't know what to say to him, he was on edge.

Later on that day people started calling and dropping by. His brother had told his mother what had happen the night before and that he did not like what his brother had done to me. He explained that he had been concerned for me and the girls all night. His mother and stepfather came over and his sisters and brothers also stopped by to welcome him home. When his mom got there he told her about Jr. and what had happened that morning. She told him not to worry about it, barely spoke to me and played with her granddaughters. His stepfather James told him to get his life together, and take care of his family. I could tell this went in one ear and out the other. All he wanted to do was talk about Jr. His mother said, "Look, honey, just do what James said because Bubba (Uncle Bill) doesn't want all of this confusion in his apartment. He's giving you and your family a place to stay really cheap so don't mess things up over some shit you have heard."

Things did not get any better, they got worse. My husband wanted to argue and fight every day and night. He watched every move I made and listened to my telephone conversations. If I walked down the street to the market, he would come to the market to see why it was taking me so long. He was driving me crazy and the girls were totally afraid of him as they watched everything he did. Uncle Bill told him over and over to stop this mess or he would have to move and he meant it.

When my friends called, he monitored the calls and sometimes would not let me talk. If they came over, he would tell them that I could not have company, that I had my work to do, I had to iron, wash, cook and clean and told them to stop dropping by because I was a married woman. They left after giving him a good cursing out. One of my friends, Barbara, told him that she needed to be married to him, not me. She said I was too kind, too nice, but she would kick his ass. They told me they were trying to organize the singing group again and they wanted me to sing with them. Again he interfered, telling them I could not sing with them and to get someone else. I had nothing to say. I simply couldn't go to rehearsal with them. They hated him but he didn't care. He had the control.

When my sister-in-law Trina, my brother William, or any of my relatives came to visit, which wasn't that often, he thought they were bringing messages from Jr. Jr. was really worried about me and the girls. He asked them to go and see if the girls and I were okay. I would not see Jr. anymore because I truly was trying to work things out with my husband and Jr. said he understood, but that if I ever needed him, he was there for me and he would wait forever if he had to. He said that with a guy like that he would screw up sooner or later because he had no balls.

Once my husband and I had a terrible fight and I called my cousin Rosy and her husband Willie in Los Angeles. She came and tried talking to him but got nowhere. So she told him off, letting him know that I had a family that loved me and would not stand for him abusing me. I never told Mom because I didn't want to upset her or Aunt Connie. They knew something was wrong because I didn't go to visit them as often. My family tried to stay out of our marriage because they didn't want to get involved or to take sides. I knew after two to three weeks that I wasn't going to stay with this man. It got so bad that once again I called my cousin Rosy asking this time if she and her husband Willie would please come and pick up the girls and me. She said she was on her way.

A.J. came over and said, "My grandson sure has changed. I am so sorry you are going through all of this. He is crazy." My cousin Rosy showed up with her husband to pick us up. I started packing up some things and told my husband it was over, that I could not take any more of his abuse. I told him I would pick up the rest of our things later. He called Uncle Bill, his mother and James. Uncle Bill said, "I am not surprised and I am not in it. It's all your fault. I've had to come over several times and I am sick of it." When his mother arrived she asked what was going on. I told her I was leaving. I told her that she never cared about me or about what I was going through. "All you want me to do is please your son so you don't have to deal with him, not even caring what your grandchildren are going through." Then my mother-in-law, and cousin exchanged a few choice words.

My husband had the nerve to start crying and begging. I wanted to slap his face with disgust and anger for all he had put me through. Now he claimed he wanted to do the right thing. His mother told him to stop crying and let us leave. "But this is my wife," he said. She told him shut up and let her go and you'll be fine. So I left, moving in with another cousin, Rossie and her family, in Aliso Village in Los Angeles, California.

My cousin's were so sweet and kind, always there for us. I then called Jr. and told him where I was. I asked if I could borrow some money to give my cousin for food. The next day he came with money and groceries for everyone.

My children's father moved in with his mother and kept calling and begging me to come back to him. After telephone calls and a couple of visits from him, in addition to listening to my mom and Aunt Connie, I went back to him. Terrible, terrible mistake. And I felt like a complete fool having once again to explain to Jr. that he was my kids' father and that I needed to try to make it for their sake. I was really falling in love with Jr., he was so good to me and my girls and they loved him.

My husband had found a job and his mother and stepfather rented us an apartment on Myrtle St. in Santa Ana, California. His brother Jeffrey and wife Jean lived upstairs. She and I were like sisters sharing everything. I soon became pregnant and as usual morning sickness. He had not changed a bit. He was meaner than ever starting to spank the girls for any little thing they did. If I tried to stop him, he would hit me with the belt. I really started to hate him and no one could talk to him. Even his brother Jeffrey tried talking to him, especially about how strict he was with the girls, Pamela and Regina. He told everyone to stay out of his business and leave him alone. Jean was furious but there were problems with her own marriage and she had a son of her own. My situation was worse than before. Finally I called my girlfriend Earlene. She came and we packed her car. I moved out while he was at work. I was livid with myself, my mom, my aunt, his mother and his stepfather.

My husband and I never got back together again. The girls and I stayed with mom for a minute Jr. helped me get an apartment and some furniture. I was pregnant, frustrated, and angry. I was actually in denial about being pregnant. I had gained a little weight so I thought that maybe I was just getting fat. But, boy, did I have a craving for tacos. I decided to visit my doctor, Dr. Garcia, to go on a diet and get diet pills. He knew I was distraught and in denial so he went along with me, giving me vitamins that I thought were diet pills. My third daughter continued to grow inside of me and I was getting bigger and bigger. Finally Dr. Garcia said, "Yes, my dear, you are five months pregnant. But you were so confused when you first came to see me telling me you wanted diet pills that I went along with you. Your sister Maxine and sister-in-law Jean who came in with you said to go along with you for a while." I explained to the doctor that I was tired all of the time and needed some energy. The doctor just smiled and told me that I needed some iron and gave me a prescription to take right away.

The pills made baby Debbie strong and healthy. I moved to Los Angeles for a while but Jr. talked me into coming back to Santa Ana. I rented the house next door to Aunt Connie who was very happy to have the girls and me close to her. I gave birth to Debbie Kay on August 13th and Jr. was as excited as if she was his very own child. He had seen me through the pregnancy and had bonded with the baby. He bought her entire layette and, to top things off, a car bed so he could take her for a ride everyday. Jr.

did everything for her. She was totally spoiled and only he could calm her down when she was screaming, crying, and throwing a tantrum.

Pamela started kindergarten at Franklin Elementary School in September 1962. Jr. bought all of her clothes, shoes and whatever she needed. Regina turned five December twenty-eighth of that same year, but because the cut off date for kindergarten was December fifth she could not start school that year. She sadly had to wait another year. She was crushed because she was all ready to go and be with her sister. But everything Pamela learned at school she taught to Regina, making her more advanced when she started school.

HUSBAND #2

EDGAR NATHANIEL SPENCER, JR.

Edgar Nathaniel Spencer, Jr., my best friend, my love, and my second husband. Rugged, handsome, respected and tough. Taking no crap from anyone. He made me feel special, safe and secure. My girls loved him and so did I. No one bothered him and he didn't bother anyone. He was calm and straight-forward, yet if he didn't like you, you knew it; he didn't tell others, he told you.

Jr. tried for years to take me out. My answer was always no, no. no. No, I was a getting a divorce and he had a bad reputation. He was nice, older but sexy. Finally, I said yes, o.k., after a month of dating, it was on. I let him move in with us, knowing this was not the right thing to do but he was good for us and we were so happy with him.

Jr. Spencer and I finally became an official couple. I expressed how sorry I was for everything I had put him through in the past and for getting pregnant. His answer was, "I wanted you, your unborn child, and your two daughters. I wanted to take care of all of you. You were a package deal and I wanted the whole entire package." And that's exactly what he did, took good care of us.

However, he was misunderstood by many people. They thought Jr. was bad news but I didn't care what people said or thought. He was one of the most generous and kindest men I had ever met. And he did not care what people said about him because he knew who he was. He told me not to listen to all the lies people were saying about him, that they really did not know him. And he was absolutely correct. He was wonderful to my daughters and me, and my family loved him. All except Mama and Aunt Connie. They did not trust him at first because they were believing the gossip. Later Mom and Aunt Connie said this is why you are not to judge any man. Only God could do that. "Jr. Spencer is a good man. The way he takes care of you and these children, he has proven that to be true."

My brother-in-law Jeffrey and his wife Jean split up and she had no place to go. She was from San Diego, California but did not want to go back there so she and her son moved in with us. I asked Jr. and he said, "If you want them to then the answer is yes." He loved Jean and her son and they loved him. He also fed and clothed them just like he did for us. It was as if they were his own family. This was Jr.

Although I loved Jr. very much, I didn't care for some of his friends. He was gone a lot, day and night, so I welcomed my sister-in-law and her son. I loved both of them also. The rumor was that Jr. was dealing drugs. I was in disbelief and hurt, wanting no part of this because I hated drugs. I confronted him about this telling him how frightened I was and that I would leave. Of course, he denied that he was involved with drugs. He changed his habits and got a good job because he did not want to lose us.

Jr. and I got married in 1964 at his mother Mae's house. It was a very small wedding, being his first and my second. Mae could not believe how her son had reformed. We had a small reception later at our home. We didn't care who came or approved of our marriage, we were in love. My new mother-in-law loved to cook, play cards and have fun at her house every weekend. Her relatives and friends would come over and they had so much fun. She was very good to my children, making no difference with them, treating them all the same and I loved her for this.

October 18, 1964, I gave to birth to our son, we named him Gregory Edgar Spencer. We all were so excited, well except Debbie because she had been the baby for two years. A baby in the house and a boy at that!

Oh, no my mother didn't bring a boy into this house. We always watched her around the baby. I watched her peering in on him constantly saying, "Hi, Baby," and "Stop all that crying." She had some nerve. We all spoiled my son, my boy. After three girls, I welcomed him. He was such a joy. Jr. got so disgusted with all of us females peering in on him and talking baby talk. The baby couldn't make a sound of discomfort before we were running to his bed. Jr. said, "You females are going to make a sissy out of that Cat. My son is not going to be worth a damn, a mama's boy." Did he have nerve or what? Remember how he was with Debbie? I will admit that we were a little sickening. If Jr. spanked Greg, we would cry and be totally upset with him.

Jr. and I moved to Del High on a lot with four houses. My brother and his family moved across from us. We both had front houses on the lot. Jr. and I were still very happy. However, I was still not happy with his peers. Some of them were drug addicts, dealers, or suppliers. He didn't allow them to come to our home. He demanded respect from all of his friends and often told me, "I don't deserve you, Lil' Mama (a nickname, I was also called Shorty), but I am honored to be in your life and will hurt anyone that try to hurt you. I want everyone to respect you." Sometimes his friends would forget and come by the house and Jr. would be furious. But when he got through telling them off they never dropped by again.

I went to work for a short time at my request not Jr.'s and my sister- in- law Trina watched the children. With us living so close to each other the children could sleep late and she would come to get them, making sure they ate and got dressed. When I got home from work, Debbie would run to greet me first and tell me, "Mama, Auntie Trina comb our hair so hard and tight all of us look like we are Asian. And when we are outside playing she always call one of us inside to get her Tab soda and Tareyton cigerettes. And we have to watch Dark Shadows with her. Talk to her,

Mama." Debbie would say all of this with Trina sitting right there. I would laugh so hard and so would everyone else. Trina would tell her "I am going to spank you, Debbie, and break your back." Of course she did not mean it literally. It was a saying Trina always said to all the children, when they were out of control. I am going to break your back.

Our two families always had fun things to do: a party, barbeque, or a picnic at the park. We would invite our sister Maxine and her family, and other relatives and friends. Jr.'s favorite word was shit. Not just shit, but shiiiitt. Then he would crack up laughing at the way he sounded causing everyone else to laugh because he said it with meaning, real slow.

Not only did Jr. give me respect, he gave me space, material things, money and most of all love. And he was very protective. He was like a godfather to many friends and family. They came to him for advice, knowledge and respected what he said. He was intelligent, streetwise, and blunt, telling it like it was. Jr. loved his relatives and had such a hearty laugh. When he laughed, everyone around him would laugh, not even knowing what the joke was about, or what he was saying. He loved to play cards, a game called bid whiz, with his brothers Wilbert and Henry. They would run a Boston, meaning they would get all the books, not allowing the other players to get one book. When he and Wilbert were partners, they would speak pig Latin and piss everyone off because others thought they were cheating, and most of the time they were. He had a special friend and cousin name Nova that everyone called Sis. She loved Jr. like a son and he loved her like a mother. Her daughter Betty was closer than a cousin, they were like sister and brother. Sis and Betty were always there for him and very protective. He loved them both and had great respect for both. He and his brother Wilbert took Betty to parties and concerts and dared any guy to get out of line with her. Jr. also had a great love for my brother and sister who were more than in-laws, they were friends. Trina felt she could trust Jr. with her deepest secrets.

Jr. loved to see me dance and hear me sing. He especially enjoyed watching me get ready for church. He was always telling me, "Don't be late, Mama. I don't go but you have enough religion for both of us. That's why I love you so much. Please pray for me." He had told me some horror stories about his life. He explained how he had become confused when his dad and mom split up. His mom had taken the oldest son Henry, leaving him and Wilbert with their dad. His dad, having to work, would leave them with Miss Van. This woman, who he called a witch, had no children of her own and hated kids. His dad did not know this at the time. They went hungry most of the time, ragged and dirty. She beat him all the time with chains and hangers. She would tie him up in a chair or onto the bed and wouldn't let him go to use the bathroom. If he wet the bed, not only would she beat him, she would make him suck the urine from the sheets. She made Jr. get up at 4:00am to peel potatoes for her roomers. She hated Jr., but wasn't that way with his brother Wilbert.

Jr.'s dad would be out of town for months. He trusted Mrs. Van and believed she was taking care of his sons. When Jr. told me this, I cried for days. I was hurting for him and his brother Wilbert, but especially for him. He said his mother knew what was happening but never came to see what was going on with her sons or take them away from this. Finally their dad found out what was going on and cursed Miss Van out. He took his sons away to Stockton where he met and married Jr.'s stepmother, Delia. At an early age, he left home and met an older woman who gave him money, bought his clothes and everything else he wanted or needed. She turned him onto marijuana and heroin, and he soon became entrapped with the woman and drugs.

In spite of all this, he managed to finish high school and two years of junior college. He was a whiz in math and always helped the children with their homework. We were on one accord until the craving for drugs came back and he became weaker and weaker for it. Finally I threw up both hands. I was not strong enough to compete; the drugs won and we broke up. I took my children and moved to Los Angeles. Prior to moving, I had major surgery and had accepted a position with Allstate Insurance Company. This was in 1969. My sister-in-law Jean had already moved to Los Angeles and found an apartment and put a deposit on it for me in a wonderful area.

Jr. didn't know I was moving. When he found out I had left, he was devastated. I gave my brother permission to give him a telephone number where I could be reached. He called me at my cousin's and sent money for all the kids, not just Gregory. It was a while before I let him know where I was living. We got back together, it was never the same. So we finally let go. We remained best friends, and never stopped loving each other.

When I finally met someone else and got remarried, it almost killed Jr. He was not expecting this even though he had gotten involved with another woman. We were apart for 13 years and one day I got a call from a mutual friend telling me that Jr. was very ill. I called his mother's home to see how he was doing and to my surprise she said he was there with her. He had just gotten out of the hospital and was living with her. He wasn't doing well at all, he had emphysema. I asked if he felt like having a visitor and he answered yes with excitement in his voice. I hurried over arriving at Mae's with sadness and excitement in my heart.

Jr. was laying in bed with an oxygen tank to help him breathe. I wanted to cry but I didn't want him to see me doing that so I smiled and hugged him. He smiled and said, "Hey, Mama, it's good to see you and lit up like a Christmas tree." We just stared at each other and tears started to roll down each of our cheeks. We held hands and talked and I could tell he was getting tired. He said he wasn't but it was time for me to leave. Leaving him was one the hardest things I have ever done in my life. He became sad again and told me to say hello to all the children and thanked me for coming. I told him that he didn't have to thank me for coming. "I would have been there sooner if I had known. I promise I will see you again on the weekend." He was o.k. with that. I asked if he needed anything else and he answered that he needed me.

Well, as you can imagine, I cried all the way back to Carson. When I got home, I called all the children and the rest of the family and told them how sick Jr. was and to go see him right away.

I went back as promised on the weekend and much to my surprise he looked much better. He thanked me for contacting everyone; he had been receiving a lot of visits and phone calls. My marriage to husband number three was on shaky ground so I moved and filed for my divorce in October 1988. I moved in with my daughter Debbie in Long Beach, continuing to see Jr., helping to take care of him. We got an apartment in Long Beach together and we were both very happy again. We lived on the third floor but had an elevator, so this was fine with Jr. in spite of his breathing condition. Later I bought a condo in Santa Ana because that's where all of his doctors were located and he needed to be close to them just in case.

Everyone was happy that I was there for Jr. and that we were together once again. It was drugs and fast living that put him in bad health. But I was willing to put my life on hold to take care of him because I could never forget how he had been there for my girls and me. I felt that if I owed anyone in this world, it was him.

Jr. gave a new meaning to jazz. It seems as though he invented it. He would sit or lie down and take long trips with Nina, Billie, Miles, Sarah, Ella, Nancy, and many other jazz artists. He definitely would zone out listening to Kenny. He would sit for hours at a time, meditating and thinking, and we knew not to disturb him.

Jr.'s health never got any better and he died August 1992. On the morning of his death, we prayed together and Jr. asked God for forgiveness of all his sins. Then we said the Lord's prayer together. I still grieve for Jr. and I will never forget my love. To the man that taught and gave me so much, find rest, find peace; no more beatings, no more goodbyes. You were my best friend and my rock.

HUSBAND #3

I was introduced to Mister by my friend Mattie in the seventies after Jr. and I had split up. He was a local bus driver. All the drivers ate at a little place called Honey's Café where Mattie was the waitress. I was eating their one day and he inquired about who I was and wanted to know more about me. When I left, he gave Mattie all his information on a piece of paper: his phone numbers at work and home. I threw it away. Later in the week he asked my friend why I had not called him. Mattie told him she had given me the piece of paper and that was all she could do.

Several weeks later I saw Mister at the store around the corner from my house. He asked me why I had never called him. I asked if he was married. His reply was, "It's a long story. I am divorced but living with my ex-wife to help out with my kid's only. But I'm in the process of moving out again." He was buying a bottle of bourbon, which should have been my clue to walk on by, but no, I shared with him that I was also recently separated. He smiled and asked if he could call me sometime. I said sure, I guess so, but only after you moved out. I told him to give his telephone number to my friend Mattie when he was on his own and only then would he be able to get mine.

Mister eventually contacted Mattie after a couple of weeks asking her to let me know that he had moved out and was staying with his sister Patsy. He gave her his new number to pass on to me and asked for me to call him as soon as possible. When I finally called he wanted to take me out to dinner or a movie. I was feeling a little lonely so I thought what the heck. He seemed to be a really nice guy, and very good looking, so I took a chance. We started to date regularly and I began to like him. I thought it was time for him to meet the significant others in my life, my children.

My two older children were fourteen and fifteen and could care less about my love life. They were attending Crenshaw High School. My nine-year old daughter flipped out but my son who was seven said that whatever I did was fine with him. Deborah never accepted my relationship with him and she not only told me, she told him also. I ignored my daughter's objections and got more involved with him. Mister had gotten his own apartment but would occasionally stay over at our house.

He had three wonderful children and another one on the way by another woman. Mister was from a large family and I loved them all. And felt I was accepted by all of them. He was jealous of the rapport I had with his family which I did not understand. I told him that I thought he would be happy that we got along so well. I loved and accepted his children and they, me. But we had a problem with the other woman at first because she was still in love with him. But after several months, she accepted the fact that he was with someone else.

About this time, I began having problems with my daughters and gangs. We lived in one gang territory, the Brims, and one of my daughters was dating a guy that lived in another gang territory, the Crips. I was told all this because I never understood this gang thing. This was all frightening and confusing. I was so worried and afraid for my teenage daughters but Mister was not moved by these gang threats. He said he dealt with them every day. He also grew up around gangs in Watts.

When Mister asked me to marry him, I was somewhat relieved. He said he wanted to take care of us and move us to a home in another part of Los Angeles County. We moved into a 4-bedroom home in Carson, California with wonderful neighbors. The wedding day came and I had this deep feeling to call it off. There was doubt in my mind, something, I call the Holy Spirit told me to think about what I was getting into, that I would not be happy and that I would be sorry for the rest of my life.

Of course, I ignored everything I was hearing or feeling. I proceeded to get dressed and get my wedding over with, at my cousin Rosie's house. All of my relatives and guests were waiting, even the minister was already there. I was two hours late. I arrived with all the children, his and mine, and we were all depressed. My daughter Deborah was livid. Mister was angry and started yelling about us being so late. We said our vows until death do us part, and I died a thousand times in that marriage. Everything started when we moved into the new house.

Mister was wonderful until we moved and got married. On day one he had a family meeting on how to run the garbage disposal, the dishwasher, and so on. It was as if we had never had any modern facilities before. He changed drastically and was jealous and mean. He didn't want my relatives, friends, or the kid's friends to come over. Mister had terrible mood swings and started to drink heavily. I was torn between my kids and my husband. He wanted to know who was first in my life. "I bet your kids come before me," he would say. I told him, "God is first and I think you know the rest."

If my friends or family came over, he would not come out of the bedroom, not even to speak. I would be livid and embarrassed and would make excuses for his rudeness. My kids were furious with me for staying with him and in that kind of relationship. We started arguing almost every night. I would argue with him and then stop but he would continue on for hours. I thought me shutting up would make him shut up but it seemed as though it gave him more power. My children resented me for not saying anything back to him, not realizing that if I did, it only made things worse. I also began taking his dinner to the bedroom on a tray day after day, regardless if we had fought or not. My friends and kids asked me how

I could work, come home, cook and take his dinner to him. They thought I was crazy. I tried to explain that you could not change in the middle of the stream. It would cause more trouble for me to stop this routine because he expected this. He had already put his bluff in and the fear of him was already in me and he knew it. I was afraid of him and I didn't want him to say anything to my children.

Mister made everyone uneasy. This is why I started taking his dinner to the bedroom so that the kids could eat in peace. They didn't understand telling me how much they resented him. "Why do you let him talk to you like that?" He was extremely jealous of my son. If Greg would lay on me and watch television, he got angry. If I helped the kids with their homework, he would argue about that. I was embarrassed to go outside. My kids also resented him for being so mean and evil and resented me for being weak because I allowed this man to belittle me and take away my pride and dignity. He made me insecure and withdrawn. We broke up and got back together many times.

One weekend my children and I moved in with one of his sisters. She had been in our house when he went off and could not take the verbal abuse he was giving us. My neighbors felt sorry for my kids and me because they had heard and seen what was going on. I could see the pity in their faces and anger in their conversation. I loved all my neighbors. His ex-wife Marvel, was very nice and thanked me for being nice to her children, for buying them gifts, school clothes, or anything that I thought they needed.

Mister's son got into some trouble and, when released moved in with us. During his stay with us he was killed on our front lawn. Mister actually blamed me for his death. He told me that he wished it had been me or one of my kids that had died. That hurt and things were never the same with us. Mister continued to accuse me of letting his son die. Since I was at home when it happened, he would have me tell him over and over again, day after day, night after night, how it all happened.

I was especially tormented when we went into the bedroom at night. My kids would listen at the door to make sure he didn't hit me. Prior to his son's death, my two oldest girls had moved out. They could not take anymore of this hell house, so with my blessings they moved. My youngest daughter Deborah said she would never leave me. She was the one he wanted out because she would always take up for me. He was mean to all of my children but I couldn't leave because I didn't have the money to rent a place. I didn't have first and last months rent nor all the money it would take to get started again. He knew this whenever I moved he would beg me back and make promises he never intended to keep. I believed his lies.

When Deborah left, Greg and I caught hell, because he hated my son, because he knew we all loved Greg's father, Jr. And Jr.'s name could not be mentioned, nor was he allowed to call. I finally helped Greg get his own apartment. I knew it was time for Greg to leave because one night I got up to get a glass of water and found him laying on the floor in the living room crying. He was confused and hurt. He asked me, "Mama, why does he treat you like that? You are so good and kind and treat everyone good. You're a good Christian woman and I hate him and I am going to kill him if he ever hits you again. How can you take this Mama? I love you and don't want anyone to mistreat you ever. It's not right, and he should not be allowed to live and just treat people any way he wants to and get away with it. He thinks everyone is afraid of him.

I didn't know what to say. I was scared to stay in the room too long and I was afraid to let Mister hear me consoling my son. I hugged and kissed my son and went back into the bedroom to cry all night. I knew I had to get my child out of this mess and soon. My son started to drink at age 15. He was devastated over not being with his dad or accepted by my husband. My son started hanging out and drinking a lot with other kids in the neighborhood. My poor son was lost. His sisters did what they could to help him do the right thing. His younger sister would even fight his battles for him and then kick his butt for getting her involved.

Mister was all business and a good provider. He had A-1 credit. He did not believe in a lot of bills, and the ones he had were paid on time. I always admired this about him that he was better with the finances than he was with relationships. He was also a womanizer. A big flirt. And had no respect when it came to flaunting it in my face. He even gave women our home phone number and told them it was okay to call. When I would question him about this he would say he was grown and not to question him. A couple of the women told me very boldly that he told them to call him. I was hurt and angry. Hurt because he did not love and respect me enough to at least be discreet. Angry because I allowed the devil to bring Mister into our lives. I married him for better or worse, but now I wanted out. I prayed a lot and trusted that God would deliver me from this nightmare. I said to the Lord, "I know you forewarned me and I should not be praying about a divorce. I married for better or worse but help me out of this anyway please, Lord."

I washed and iron his clothes and he would have a couple of drinks, turn on the shower and throw all the ironed clothes in the shower. He would then demand that I pick them all up. No way. Sometimes when I would bring his dinner to him, he would throw the plate against the wall and tell me he didn't want that shit. "What are your kids eating? Steak?" I would tell him that we are all eating the same thing. He would slap me and say, "Who in the F--- do you think you are talking to b----?" I didn't know what to do. Sometimes I would fight back but a woman is no win with a man, and if I screamed, my kids would come running. If I cried, my children would see my eyes when I would take his plate back into the kitchen. They watched me closely when he was home. My oldest daughter Pamela would stay in the hallway and listen for any sudden movements, loud noises, loud voices or my scream. Sometimes she stayed up all night, it was driving her crazy. She started staying in her room a lot, listening to sad music with the lights out. Regina stayed away as much as possible with her boyfriend. She hated coming home because the tension in the house made her real nervous. She would come home as late as possible and go to bed. Deborah became more and more resentful and protective. She was confused and bitter because I put all of them into this horrible pit and would not take them out of it for good.

I had friends to tell me that they would leave this man and never look back or kill him. "He's horrible and I don't know why or how you stay with him." Even his own family did not like coming around. When he drank he talked a lot about his childhood and the things that had happened to him. We attended different churches. I thought it would be better if we went to the same church so I joined his church. It was a family church, almost everyone there was related and obviously he had said some negative things about me to his family because the congregation was not very receptive of me in the beginning. I joined the choir and the pastor and congregation really enjoyed my singing. The pastor was impressed with my singing, so I did solos and lead.

The pastor and the rest of his family got really close to me and my children. So close that the pastor began to notice Mister's attitude towards me. One Sunday after church he asked me if there was a problem and if he could help. I told him everything and he told me he could feel my pain in my singing. My singing was from the soul and the message was so sad and strong that it touched everyone in the church. The pastor said I had a ministry in my singing that set the congregation on fire. He wanted me to sing a pastoral song before he came to the pulpit to bring the message almost every Sunday, God's amazing grace.

He was a good preacher and a wonderful person; he had a lovely, wonderful wife, who I also loved, and a beautiful daughter who had a beautiful speaking and singing voice. Pastor felt that Mister and I should come for marriage counseling. He had married us and felt even then that there was a problem. He said I should have said something then. Mister and I started our counseling with the pastor and our relationship went from good to bad to worse. It got to the point that the pastor invited me and my family to move in with his family. "I never realized you were going through all of this. I am so upset with your husband, I don't even want to see him and I know this is not the Christian way, or the way of a pastor. How do you put up with this? My prayers are with you and my heart goes out to you and those children. My invitation is still open. He won't even listen to reason or to anyone; it's almost impossible to talk to him. There is no reasoning or understanding him."

The choir would fellowship over to each other's house once a month. This particular Sunday was my Sunday to have them over. We would all potluck. I could tell they really didn't want to come, but they did not want to hurt my feelings. Well, as it turned out, they should have hurt my feelings because all hell broke loose.

Mister called home to see if they were there and I told him yes. I asked if he was coming home to fellowship with us. He was the manager of his dad's business and he could leave for a little while if he wanted to. He said no and I asked why not. "Come on, no one ever comes to our house and there are men here also." Mister said not to ask him any questions and to just forget it. One half hour later he pulled up into the driveway like a mad man, jumped out of the van, and stormed into the house. He grabbed my arm, took me into the bedroom and slapped me as hard as he could, stating don't ever question me again. I screamed and all the kids jumped in. He came out telling all of my guests to leave, just get out. My guests were in shock. Words cannot explain my embarrassment and hurt. We tore up the house fighting. The police were called and the kids and I moved. Mister once again begged me into coming home. "I don't know what got into me. I swear things will be different and I will go to counseling."

This was the third time I had packed up my children, took them out of school, and moved. This time he promised it would be different. He wanted to talk about opening a business. I was very hesitant but he convinced me it would be a good investment. I found out later he had talked a girlfriend into forging my name on a loan for a charter bus just in case I refused.

We purchased the bus and it was again one of the biggest mistakes I've ever made. Mister started making runs to Reno, Las Vegas and any place he could get a charter, in state or out of state, as far as Arkansas and New Orleans. Later I found out that he took a different woman with him on every trip. He didn't let me know anything about his business, I just helped with the cleaning and preparations for the next trip. On one occasion he and I met the nicest elderly lady who wanted to charter the bus to Arkansas. I went with him to pick up the deposit and she and I bonded like mother and daughter.

Mama D., that's what I called her, didn't know he was married because she had seen some things he had done. She was very upset with him, and she said she was going to tell him so. Mister was running women like cattle and he became more and more disrespectful. He became mean and vicious so I moved out one more time and stayed with my cousin Connie in Inglewood. By this time, all of my children had moved away so I didn't have to worry about uprooting them again. I said, "This is it! You can have the house and furniture, and I am out of here."

My cousin Connie was wonderful. She made me feel very welcome and secure as always. She didn't want to take any money but I insisted on giving her something and to do all the cooking. This was fine with Connie because she didn't like to cook. Meanwhile, my mom had surgery and was living with my sister. I had promised Mom that she could also stay with me. I felt so sad because I was no longer living in my home and basically had no place to call my own. Mister again wanted me to come back and I agreed, on one condition, that my grandmother could move in with me on the same day I returned. He agreed.

I called mom and told her the condition under which I was going back with Mister. She said, "Are you sure, honey. I don't want to cause you any problems." I told her not to worry about it. I talked with my sister and told her I would be picking Mom up and moving back in with Mister over the weekend. My sister had taken care of Mom since her surgery and I knew that I had to help out with her rehabilitation. I had a weak stomach and I didn't think I could have given her the care she needed after her surgery.

I picked up Mom and we both moved into my home. Mister really didn't want her in our home and he made it obvious. He did little things that made her uncomfortable. His granddaughter Shona also lived with us. She loved Mom and was good to her. Eventually Shona's mother picked her up, leaving all of us sad. I took Mom to the senior citizen building in our city to get her involved, thinking this would keep her from getting so lonely while I was at work. Mom was not impressed with this arrangement. They took her picture and gave her a badge, showed her around the facility and introduced her to other seniors. Mom said, "These people make me depressed." I didn't force her to go back.

I registered with Meals-On-Wheels to make sure she had hot meals every day. I gave a key to my neighbor Connie and she let them in every day. Mister didn't like all of this attention being given to Mom. He was jealous and started complaining. I had decorated Mom's room really cute and he complained that it was stinking. He complained that he was not comfortable in his own home any more. He also complained that I spent too much time with Mom. I became angry and Mom detected his attitude. She told me she was sorry, she knew my husband didn't want her there. I explained that if she left, I was leaving with her. Mom had always been there for me and that whatever happen we were a team. Mom said, "God bless you, honey. I hear your husband every night nagging you." She didn't know how I could endure this.

One day I came home from work to find all the windows and doors open. Mom was sitting on the couch shivering, she was so cold. Mister had opened the windows and doors because he said that the house had an odor. I ran into the bedroom and attacked him asking why did he do such a terrible thing. "It's freezing in here and Mom is shaking from being so cold. You should be ashamed of yourself. My mom doesn't smell because I keep her room clean and disinfected. Maybe you are the one that is stinking." I was angry and hurt and for once I didn't care what he might do to me. I was surprised that he only gave me a dirty look.

I went back into the room with Mom and massaged her legs, put her to bed and made sure she had plenty of blankets on her. All I could do was cry and pray to God that I be delivered from all of this soon. At that very second, all the love I had ever had for this man left. I also prayed and asked God to take away the hate.

On Sunday I took Mom to 8:00am services at church and dropped her off. When I returned home, Mister was waiting for me. He wanted my mom gone by the time he returned from his church at 1:30pm. Yes, he went to church every Sunday. I had stopped going with him and was attending another church because I was tired of being embarrassed every Sunday after church. I was shocked at his request. In fact, I asked him if he was saying that he didn't want my mom in this house. He said she was not welcome in his house any longer and that if I didn't tell her, he would do it. The more he talked the more the bitterness and hatred grew in my soul and I started to cry. Mister didn't care about my crying. He wanted her out of his f----- house.

Mister drove off leaving me devastated and going out of my mind with pain and sadness for Mom. How was I going to break this horrible news to her? I called my children crying and screaming. They wanted to go to his church, call him outside and beat him for causing me so much grief. But most of all they wanted to beat him for wanting to put their great grandmother out. I told them no, I would call them back. I called Aunt Connie and she told me to calm down and we prayed. I told Aunt Connie that Mister wanted Mom out today. After praying she told me to tell Mom that she wanted her to stay with her for a couple of weeks and in the meantime we could work out something else. Aunt Connie said, "God is going to handle your husband. He is a cruel person and he can't continue to mistreat children and old folk and get away with it without reaping and suffering himself. I may not live to see it but I know God is going to whip him and bring him to his knees."

I picked Mom up from church and could not look her in the face. She knew something was wrong because I could not hold back the tears. I told her that Aunt Connie wanted her to stay with her for a while. She didn't want to go but she said she understood. I took her to Aunt Connie's, and I stayed for about an hour, then rushed back home, nervous and sad. When Mister came home he asked where was she and I told him she was gone.

That's what he wanted and I left the subject alone. I didn't have much to say to him in the following days. It was an effort just to speak to him. His mom called and I told her what had happened. She came over and told him he was wrong and made him feel bad, so he let me pick Mom up and bring her home. I was, however, already making plans to leave him for good.

Mom died shortly afterwards and I moved out and filed for divorce. I never looked back. Of course he wanted me back but I told him that God had once again given me my freedom and sanity and I would never come back to that hell house that had caused me and my children nothing but pain, sadness and grief.

Thank you God for the victory.

Chapter VII

CH *D* NO.

PAMELA

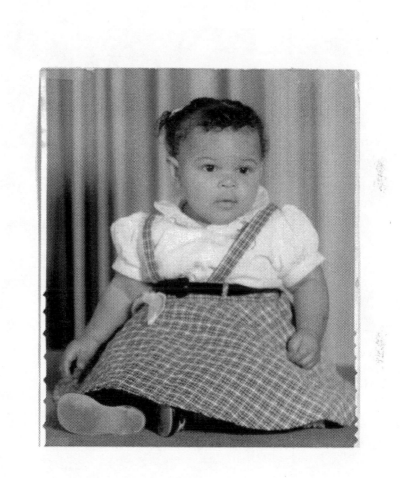

Top left:
Pamela, Pam, Pam and Bänka

Lower left:
Pam & daughter Bänka

Lower right:
Pam and Bro Greg

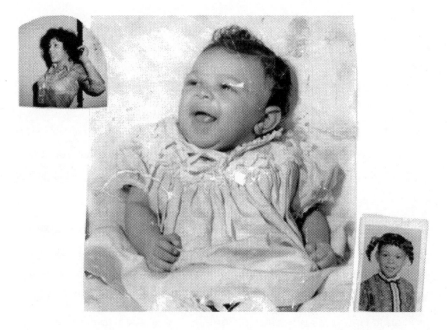

PAMELA Denise was born February 22, 1957. She was everyone's joy. She was a doll. My relatives and friends gave me an enormous baby shower and I got everything she needed: a bed, a dresser, a bassinet beautifully decorated, and her whole layette, including diaper service. I was so excited to get all of these things, and when she was born, all of my girlfriends took turns coming over to bathe her. After dressing Pamela, they took her wherever they were going.

Pamela was quiet, serious, loved to read and loved school. She didn't like cartoons, dolls, or playing house. She was Mama's little helper. She would always help me clean the house, wash and fold the laundry, and loved helping me with her little sister. She was somebody in my life, my little lady. When her sister Regina was born, ten and half months later, she was thrilled. Whenever someone gave her anything she would say, "Give one to my sister." Pamela didn't stay a baby long with her sister being born so soon after her. She was a quick learner. She was walking and talking at ten months old, and before she turned one, she was potty-trained and weaned from the bottle.

When Pamela started kindergarten, Jr. would walk her or drive her to school every morning. One day she told me, "Mom, you guys don't have to take me to school anymore or pick me up. I am a big girl." So we would walk or drive at a distance. One day we didn't go to pick her up and Pamela did not come home on time. We were worried and scared sick. We contacted everyone. The search was on and I was going out of my mind. Finally, before we called the police, we decided to go back to the school and look in her classroom and there she was asleep in a corner. The principal was furious that her teacher did not check her classroom before leaving it. Pamela said that she had been tired and decided to take a nap. We made a decision to continue taking and picking her up a little while longer.

Pamela went to Sunday School every week. She loved church, and loved to be with her godmother she called Nana. Nana was awesome.

Pamela attended junior high and high school in Los Angeles. She was not only my daughter, but also my friend. I was very young and needed her more than she knew. Pamela would help with the other children's homework, cleaning their rooms and making lunches. We had a routine of setting out all clothes and taking baths at night and she helped faithfully.

Whatever I said, she enforced it with the rest of the children. By the time Pamela reached high school she was tired of playing mama to my kids. She wanted to go to parties, school dances and on dates so she didn't have time for her younger sisters and brother. I would let Pamela and her sister Regina go to parties but I would tell them to be back at a certain time. Pamela was always back home at the specified time.

When we moved to Carson, she attended Carson High and graduated. She always had good grades, good reports from her teachers and was popular among her friends. I put a lot of trust and confidence in her. I had her on a pedestal. She hated this and one day told me that she was human just like everyone else, so please not to put her on a pedestal. She said that this attitude of mine had caused problems between she and her sister Regina. Pamela loved Regina, she and Regina were inseparable until thes age of thirteen and fourteen. They were so close in age and looked so much alike that I even dressed them alike. When they entered the teen years they asked me to please not dress them alike and I respected their request.

Pamela attended her grad night and prom. She graduated in 1975 and we bought her a 1975 Camero. Pamela attended Cerritos College taking court reporting. Her grandmother Thelma bought her a court-reporting machine. I felt bad that I was not able to carry the finances for her college education. She worked part-time and got a grant to help out. But things were so bad at home, she couldn't study or concentrate so she dropped out of college. She got a full-time job and moved out. Never forgetting about her mom, every payday she would come over and give me money just because "you deserve it." She bought me expensive gifts for birthdays, Mother's Day and Christmas.

Pamela always had a sadness about her that bothered me. When I asked her what was wrong she would say, "I am OK, don't worry about me. You have too many other things to worry about." Before she moved out, she told me she was sorry that she just could not stay at this house any longer. "This man is driving all your kids crazy. You deserve better and you belong with a man with class and intelligence. I hate the way he talks to you, he treats us like we're dogs, and when you take his food to him on a tray to the bedroom, it makes me crazy. I will never ever do this for any man. You both work and you come home to fix a full course meal. The least he could do is come and fix his own plate. But no, he sits in that room like he is king and you're the maid. Mom, why do you do this?" I explained that it was to keep him in the bedroom so he would not come out causing problems with them. Pamela said, "We can take care of ourselves. Let him come out."

Pamela has very high standards of living. When I spoke to her about this, she would tell me that this is what I had taught and instilled in them, to reach always for the best and do their best. This made me feel good because I had almost forgotten what it was like to reach; I had been down for so long. Pamela would call and check on me, never missing a day.

She was working and going to school part time. But something happened that changed all of that. She got pregnant. In the beginning, she was devastated. This could not be happening to careful Pamela, but it had. On March 28, 1988 B'anka was born, the joy of her life. Pamela never allowed the family to talk "baby talk" to her. She said she didn't want her walking around saying "gaga, googoo" like they did. Our grandparents would say to us, "Come to gango, come on to gaga," and people thought we all had speech problems.

Pamela has over 1100 books and has read all of them. B'anka also loves to read. This was a must with her; she explained that reading was very important. My daughter was disappointed that I never marched in the movement in the sixties. I told her I was too busy raising children but this was not acceptable at all. "You could have at least marched in something." My answer was never the right one.

Pamela would tell me, "Nothing is too good for my mom." That all their friends thought I was cool and that my children were lucky to have me for a mom. She said it with such pride, I felt great.

Thank you God, for blessing me with such a special daughter like Pamela.

Chapter VIII

REGINA

Anthony, Regina's Husband

Regina was the second of four children. She was born on December 28, 1957. What a doll. Yes, all mothers think this of their child. Regina was born so soon after Pamela it was a shock and a surprise. I had to accept and deal with it.

Regina loved her sister "Pom", this is how she pronounced her name, and wanted to do everything like her sister. Pamela taught Regina everything that she had learned in and out of school. They were inseparable. Regina always said, "Give me some for my sister Pom." If complimented, she said, "Thank you. Pom too."

Regina was beautiful and was told this quite often. It started to concern me because I didn't want her to be conceited. She did have long, beautiful hair and I dressed her cute. With all this, she looked even prettier. Of course, me being Mom, I was proud to say she was my little girl.

From an early age, Regina loved television. I gave the girls breakfast, dressed them and turned on the cartoons because it would be too early to play outside. Regina could sit there for hours whereas Pamela would get bored and find a book to read. Regina never moved. She would look and smile all day, if I allowed her to. When she watched television, everything else was blocked out. Pamela would ask her to help clean their room and Regina would say, "No, shut up, Pom. Come watch television." Their father was also a television watcher.

Regina did some modeling when she was six years old for an agency in Laguna Beach. Her picture was used on calendars and posters, showing children of all races playing together. She loved romantic and sexy movies; Ginger Rogers, Fred Astaire, and Marilyn Monroe were some of her favorite actors. Marilyn was her favorite she even started acting like her. When we couldn't take this any longer, I brought it to her attention so she could do a reality check. She did and it was better for awhile.

When Debbie was born, Regina loved her little sister, but had no patience or tolerance for her loud crying. Regina would say, "Come on, baby." But when Debbie would not stop crying, even if she gave her a bottle or toys, she would tell her, "Oh, shut up, baby," and leave her crying in a hurry, covering her ears.

As Regina got older, I noticed that she loved to party, dress sexy, and tease the boys. It was a look-but-don't-touch sort of thing. She did turn the heads of many males. I also noticed that she liked men that she could slightly control and this concerned me. She dated a very nice guy in Carson who, we all loved and I thought was marriage material, but eventually they grew apart and went their separate ways. This surprised and sadden me.

Other guys she dated were o.k., but none like my Ozzie. Some I liked and some I didn't but she was her own person and I tried to stay out of her men business.

Regina and Pamela went to modeling school in Los Angeles and they were very good. Regina was in the finals and we were very proud of her. She graduated from Carson High and when I wasn't able to buy her a new car, she was devastated. This made me sad also. She didn't understand that my marriage was on the rocks and that my financial situation had changed a lot. I bought her a bedroom set and a hope chest but this was not acceptable. She cried and threw a tantrum. A couple of months later, a deal on a car came through and I was able to buy her a used Fiat convertible from a friend. This was her first car and she loved it. Regina loved having the top down with the wind blowing through her hair. She said this made her feel free. Sadly, the car was stolen and she had no insurance. Her insurance had been canceled days before it was stolen and again devastation set in.

Regina dated a guy who played in a band. His name was also Ozzie and I liked him also. I told my daughter that he was a very nice man and that she needed to think about settling down. He played the bass guitar in the James Band. She traveled with him and the band to Buffalo, New York, when she returned to Los Angeles, she got a job and her own apartment.

Regina also had her own special love and concern for me. She stayed busy and away so she would not see everything that was going on. If I needed anything, she was there for me. She bought me my first pair of glasses and was so proud to do this for me. Whenever she found out I needed anything concerning my health, it would scare her. She would say,

"Oh my God, my poor Mother." She once told me, "Mom, I can't stand your husband. You deserve better. I hate the way he treats you. The reason I stay gone is because I will hurt him if I ever see him hit you. In fact, I hate him."

Regina was more daring than Pamela. If I let them go to a party, I would say, "Girls, I am letting you go, but you have to be home by twelve." If they ran late Regina would say to Pamela, "We are already late and in trouble so we might as well stay later." Pamela would leave her at the party and she came home hours later. She would be at their window knocking quietly, pleading for one of her siblings to let her in. If they were pissed off at her for any reason, they would say no and come to get me. She would get a spanking or be on punishment for a month. She didn't care and would tell her sister it was worth it.

Finally, my child settled down. I guess she got tired of the bright lights and the big city. Regina met her husband Anthony in Los Angeles and married him in San Jose. I was livid because I wanted my children to have a church wedding and I wanted to be a part of it, helping out wherever needed. But that was her decision to do it her way. They moved back to Santa Ana and while living there, she had to have surgery. Regina doesn't have any children as of yet. She has been pregnant but had miscarriages. She loves her nieces and nephews who call her Auntie GeeGee. They love her. My daughter loves living up north and wants me to come and live there also, so it can just be she and her mama.

Again, God, I give you all the thanks for blessing me with a special daughter like Regina. God grant me the serenity to accept the things I cannot change, the courage to change the things I can and the wisdom to know the difference.

Regina and Anthony; Baby Robert and Regina; Regina and Anthony

Chapter IX

DEBORAH

John and Deborah
Prom Picture

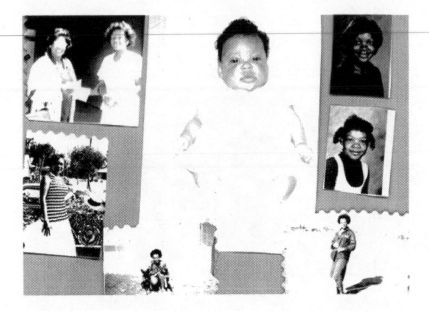

Top Left: Grandma Carrie & Debbie at Curtis Jr.'s Graduation

Deborah and my dog Chelsea; Deborah and her son
Robert
Center; Big Robert (Robert's father)
Lower left: Pam, Regina, Debbie (seated)

Right Lower: Debbie getting award at school (college)
Greg, Pam, Bänka, Robert (son) John and me
Bottom right: Pam, Baby Robert, and Greg

Debbie and son Robert

Deborah was born on August 13, 1962, five years after Pamela and Regina. She was a daddy's girl and a mama's brat, spoiled and determined. Deborah was not Jr.'s daughter biologically, but no one would have thought differently. Jr. had a way with her. She was his "boo" and he took charge of her. Jr. bathed her, took her for all her shots, and even bought a car bed, not a car seat, so he could take her for rides and she could sleep. Deborah was his joy and my cross; as far as I was concerned, she was rotten. He didn't want me to even spank her. Of course, I did what I had to do.

Deborah didn't like being around a lot of people, but she watched everything I did and imitated me. Her sisters had a hard time dealing with her because she was so spoiled. There was a special song we loved to hear her sing, Skylark. She would listen to Jr. playing his jazz and could sing like Sarah, Nancy or anyone she heard. But her favorite song was Skylark. People would pay her to sing or imitate other people. Jr. encouraged her to sing, and to charge people, smiling, he would say that's by boo. Depending on her mood, she would make a lot of money. She was only three or four years old. Where he got the name Boo from I don't know. Deborah would sing her heart out, but imitating was her specialty. My friend Wanda's husband would pay her twenty-five cents every time she would talk like her Aunt Trina.

Two years later something happened that changed her life. Gregory, her baby brother, was born. "Oh, no, not a boy! He will ruin everything!" She didn't like that baby and told everyone just how she felt about having a boy around the house. I would watch her peering in on him from time to time. As they got older she became very protective of him.

Debbie lost interest in school sometimes during the time I couldn't make up my mind if I was going to leave Mister for the last time. Moving from L.A. to Orange County and back again, checking her in and out of school.

She also felt as if she always had to protect me by being home or just being there for me just in case. Sometimes she went to a party just to get out of the house, but made sure she never stayed long and that I always knew how to get in touch with her. She was always there for me. She would be furious with her sisters for not being at home more in case I needed help. I felt terrible that she felt obligated to be my protector.

Deborah starting dating Robert, a really nice young man that she had met. They dated for awhile and on the 18th day of March, 1983 they had my grandson Lil' Robert. We were all devastated when she got pregnant because she was the baby girl and we had big plans for her and college, especially Pamela. But what a handsome little baby boy she had. This was my first grandchild and I really was excited. Deborah and baby Robert lived with us for a while and amazingly, Mister became very attached to Robert. Debbie hated this and they soon moved to their own apartment but would come to visit often.

Unfortunately, Daddy Robert, and Debbie broke up, they just could not get it together and I really liked him a lot. We all slowly moved back to Orange County. When Jr. died, Deborah almost had a nervous breakdown. She was devastated. A part of her died with him. She said Jr. was the only person in the world that understood her and she could always be truthful and straight with him. She said she could talk to him about her deepest darkest secrets.

Deborah has a testimony that will make you start thanking God every day for just being alive. Deborah was supposedly in her bedroom one night in 1980 when I received a phone call from the emergency room at Gardena Memorial Hospital. The voice on the other end was the doctor in charge. "Are you Deborah Reeve's mother?" I said, "Yes, I am." "She's been in a terrible auto accident." I could not believe what I was hearing. I quickly said, "No, you have to be kidding! My daughter is in her room. Can you hold on for a minute please?" I ran to her room and much to my surprise she was not there. I ran back to the phone and said I would be right there. I quickly summoned her sisters to come and go with me. Mister did not move or ask any questions about what was going on or if my child was okay. This was definitely another strike against him.

When I arrived at the emergency room, I was met by the doctor and he said that it looked worse than it was. She had been given something for the pain but she kept repeating, "If I don't die, my mom is going to kill me. She thought I was in my room." I walked into her room with her sisters and she started to cry and kept repeating, "I am so sorry, Mom, please don't be angry." I told her that I was not angry, just in shock because I thought she was in her room. It had been raining and a car ran the red light, crashing into the car that she was in, throwing her onto the asphalt intersection. She had a huge hole in her thigh, all you could see was white flesh. There was a gash in her arm and she had another gash over her eye. Blood was everywhere. I almost fainted but I knew I had to be strong for her. The doctor explained that they were going to graft skin from other parts of her body to repair her thigh and stitch her eye and arm.

The next day before visiting hours Jr. was at the hospital sitting by her bed. Someone had contacted him that morning and he wanted to know why we had not called him the night of the accident. He said it did not matter that we were not together. "Dot, please let me know if anything happens to any of these kids. I love them." He looked as if he had been crying and I apologized. Deborah healed from this trauma with lots of prayers and the concern and loving help of my neighbors. Martha, one of my neighbors, was a nurse. She came over to help me every day.

Six years later in 1986 the Devil tried to rob me of this same daughter. She was at a club with one of her friends in Long Beach when a guy came up to the car window. He pointed a gun in her direction and shot into the car, hitting Deborah in the mouth. Per the police, the guy was aiming at her friend, the driver of the car. Debbie's friend had words with the guy prior to the girls leaving the club. My child was rushed to Long Beach Memorial Hospital. This time I was called by a police officer. He said, "I am officer

(I can't even remember his name), calling about our daughter, Deborah Reeves. She has been shot and is at Long Beach Memorial Hospital in stable condition."

This time I composed myself as much as possible and called every prayer warrior I knew, including pastors. I also called my best friend Linnie. She was so upset by the news. She told me that she and her husband would meet me at the hospital. Her husband was a praying Christian man and already there when I got to the room where Debbie was. Again, Jr. was there standing at the side of the bed and looking down at her. Debbie didn't want to have surgery until I got there. Blood was everywhere but I knew there was hope because I totally trusted in my God. Remember who I had called on before I left home? I had no doubt that as bad as it looked that she would be fine. And again, Mister did not budge. He just lay there and watched me.

Deborah again came through this. I told her, "Honey, you need to let the whole world know how good God is, how he has spared your life again and again. God has something for you to do in this life. I don't know what it is, that is between you and God." She went to church as soon as she was able and stood up and gave a testimony about the goodness of God and how her life had been spared twice. She thanked all the people who had been praying for her and when she finished there was not a dry eye in the church. She also thanked God for a praying mother.

Deborah took the test for the State in 1990 and was called to work in 1992 right after Jr. died. She was very upset about this because she wanted to share this joy with him. He was always telling her to be patient and wait on God who was going to do something special for her. Deborah remembered all the morals and values that I had taught all of my children and was constantly reminding her siblings of them. She would remind them, "Mom raised all of us the same and I remember everything she taught us." Little things like change your linen and towels weekly; pay your bills on time; always keep your living room, kitchen, and bathroom presentable because you never know who might stop by. Even though you're invited out for holidays, always cook at home, so that when you return you have food. Be independent, but always put God first in everything you do, and you will never go wrong.

I thank God for having spared my daughter's life, time and time again; for protecting her from seen and unseen danger; for blessing me with a special daughter and friend.

Chapter X

GREGORY, MY SONNIE, MY BABY

J----- --·- -

Lower left: Greg and me at his graduation (Carson High); Center: Greg, Regina, William;' Right: Sally, Wm, Debbie; Lower left: Greg; Group: Greg, Chris, Vincent, Earl (Stupping down).

Fourth pic over: Vincent (cousin), Greg, David (Cousin); Center: Greg and his (sons) Christopher and Donte; Right: Same sons.

Gregory was born on October 18, 1964. My baby boy, my son. After having three girls, my family was complete. Gregory was so beautiful, everyone loved and spoiled him. Jr. resented this. He was always telling me, "Stop spoiling him, Mama." Jr. loved his son and he was a proud dad, spoiling him in his own way not to bring any attention to it.

We were all overly protective of Gregory. When he hurt I literally hurt. We were so foolish when it came to him. Once Jr. was trying to cut his hair and was totally messing up because Greg would not keep still. We were sitting in a line on the floor saying, "Be still, Man-Man." He started to cry and Jr. gave him a little pop with the comb. We all started crying and begging his dad to let him up because we couldn't take anymore. I would grab him out of the chair and we would all run out of the house as if Jr. was killing him. Jr. would tell us to bring him back so he could finish and I would tell him no way. "I was taking him to the barbershop." And that's what I did.

Jr. was angry but what could he do with four females and a spoiled baby boy. My brother often told me to "Stop interfering when Jr. chastises his son. You are wrong, and you are going to be sorry one day." Jr. kept telling me, "Dot, you and the girls are ruining my son. He will never be a strong man. You women need to back off and let him have a few scratches and bruises." So we did, and he did get the scratches and bruises.

Gregory stayed around his sister Pamela. He followed her everywhere and would get in her bed at night to go to sleep. He would cry after her. He loved Regina also, but around Regina he had to be quiet. "Man-Man, Regina is watching television, OK?" Debbie simply did not want to be bothered with him; he got on her nerves. She would fight him and he would tease and fight her. He pushed her into the heater and she pushed him into the heater. She would get in trouble and say, "You see everything do, but you never see what he does to me."

Greg was tough. When he got a spanking he very seldom cried. My sister-in-law, Trina said, "Let me spank him; I bet he'll cry." I did, she did, and he did. But the minute she left the room, he would tell her son David (Pee Wee) that didn't even hurt, and would start laughing. One day Trina heard him and went back to finish the job. Greg never bragged about it not hurting again.

When Gregory was three years old, everyone was working or in school. We needed a babysitter and Ko, a Korean lady who loved Gregory, offered to keep him. He loved Ko. She had a huge German shepherd that would help take care of him. When he was five years old we moved to L.A. What a mistake it was to take him from his dad. He loved his dad. I told him we had to leave for awhile because Daddy needed his space and I needed a change. I explained that Dad and I still loved each other and would one day straighten things out and get back together, but he was too young and didn't understand, but seemed to accept this.

We moved on Cochran Avenue and had a wonderful landlord who was a minister. He was wonderful with Gregory. My sister-in-law Jean had a friend that lived down the street from me and offered to babysit Gregory since their son went to the same school. D. Bean would pick him up and take him home with her until Pamela and Regina got home from school.

Mr. Homes, my landlord, spent a lot of time with Gregory, taking him to Sunday School and church every Sunday. Sometimes we all would go. Mr. Homes was the best landlord I've ever had. He was kind and a good Christian man. When we moved, it broke his heart. His wife for some foolish reason was jealous of Mr. Homes relationship with my son, so

Mr. Homes and I agreed it would be best for us to move. But Mr. Homes gave me two months free rent. I never explained to Gregory why we had to move.

We moved to Hoover Avenue and got up every morning at 4:30 am. We would start our day in the bathroom, eat breakfast, make lunches and head to the babysitter on the R.T.D. My car was not working. Greg and Debbie would be dropped off on Western at Mrs. Berdumas, the sitter on my way to Wilshire Boulevard. Pamela and Regina only went a short distance to junior high. This was our daily routine. Someimes we would all pile in the car with my cousin Maudie because she was going the same direction.

All my babysitters loved Gregory. My son could be so charming; he could make you laugh, or make you want to beat him up because he would get on your nerves. He was a clown and comedian. He was very close to his cousins and Uncle Willie, my brother. He was especially close to his cousin Pee Wee. They were inseparable. He really missed his cousin when we moved to L.A. When Gregory and all his male cousins got together, they would have a dancing and singing good time.

When we moved to another county in Los Angeles, Gregory met all the neighbors first. He wanted Mister to accept him so badly, to do all the father and son things, but it did not happen. Mister was so jealous of him being loved by us and all of the neighbors. This really confused my son, all he wanted was a dad. He was devastated and did not understand why Mister did not like him. What had he done to him to make him so bitter towards him? He didn't ask for this. I was heart broken for my son which made the girls and I even closer and more protective of him. I tried to explain to him that some men are jealous of the children's relationship with their mothers.

We also paid closer attention to Mister around my son. The girls told me that they would sometimes come into the house and Mister would be cursing and yelling at Greg. The girls would come to his defense and say something to Mister like, "I am going to tell my mother how you are talking to our little brother," but they never did.

The teacher at his elementary school would write me notes asking me to come in, that it was nothing to be alarmed about. She would explain that Greg was the class clown, cracking jokes and keeping the class amused. Even the teacher would find herself laughing with the class. Sometimes it's okay but not everyday. She asked me to speak to him about this, which I did and it soon came to a stop.

Gregory adopted one of the neighbors as a friend and dad. I am grateful to Carl for all the support and advice he gave to my son. He spent a lot of time with him. And Greg would tell him things that he never told me. I believe that God had that neighbor, on that street for my son. He helped my son to keep his sanity and I will forever be grateful to Carl.

Gregory started to ditch school and could not graduate with his class. I was furious when I found this out, but mostly hurt. My son hated to see me sad and hurt. He was hurt too and it really hit him when he saw all of his friends graduating and he wasn't. He was devastated. I told him, "Since you didn't go to school and you have no desire to go to college, you can join the military or go to work. I don't care which one you choose but you are not going to sit around here and do nothing." I had to get tough with him because he was going down the wrong side of a one-way street. I had to think and act fast. He saw that I was serious so when September was nearing, he came to me and said that he had been thinking. After seeing his friend's graduate and knowing that he should have graduated also, he wanted to go back to school and get his diploma. I told him if this is what he really wanted I would support him, but I expected him to go to school.

Gregory went to classes every day faithfully, got all the credits needed to graduate, and went to his prom and grad night with a beautiful girl. I could not afford to buy everything he needed and I did not want to let him know it was a hardship on me. I happened to share this with my supervisor JoAnne and she said, "Don't worry. I am going to buy Gregory's suit and everything he needs for graduation. Don't worry about Mister giving you a dime on it. God had put another ram in the bush, we will go to the mall on our lunch break." JoAnne spent almost two-hundred dollars and didn't want anything back. I told her she was sent by God and started to cry. She told me not to cry because it was her gift to Gregory. "You try so hard, it is my pleasure."

We were so proud of him; everyone was at his graduation except the one person that would have really made his day a success, his dad. Greg was devastated and I was livid. I called his dad and told him off. I don't believe my son ever got over that disappointment. Mister didn't go to his graduation because according to him, "You will be there with your family and friends so what do you need me there for?" His day was beautiful anyway and we were all very proud of him. We were all in tears when his name was called. We yelled, screamed, clapped, and whistled. All of his cousins were there and Greg bowed and bowed again after receiving his diploma. After graduation we all went to Trina's sister Gloria's house for a celebration. She had extended her home to us because she was like his aunt, we were all family.

After graduation he went to work for the school district as a special education trainee substitute. At first he wasn't sure if this was what he wanted to do but he continued and was very good with handicapped children. Gregory saved his money and bought a car and he was the last one to move out. My baby had grown up and cut his mother's apron strings.

While living in his apartment complex, he was introduced to his neighbor's daughter. They started dating and soon after, Christopher was born. What a handsome baby boy he was with lots and lots of thick hair. One year later guess what? Another handsome son was born. D'onte was here, and what a joy he was to the family.

August of 1992 was a nightmare for my son. He lost the one man that had meant so much to him but had never gotten a chance to share this with, his father. He wanted to let him know just how much he loved him and how he wanted to share his son's with him. He said he had so much to say to his dad and now he was gone. While Jr. lay dying that morning, I heard Gregory whispering in his ear, "Daddy, please don't leave me. Don't die. I have so much to say. We have so much to catch up on. Please don't leave me." And he was gone. Gregory was devastated and has never gotten over his dad's death.

Soon after his dad's death he met another young lady, Lori. They got married without any of his family being there and we were outraged at both of them and hurt. Our thoughts were how could he have done this. We would have helped him with a beautiful wedding. This caused bad feelings in our family for a while. His wife had a daughter named Tiffany from a previous relationship and she was beautiful. We all accepted her. Then Aaron was born, another son. He was a baby version of Jr., we were amazed. Now there is Taylor Ann, we call her Tae. Tae loves to dress up and keep everything in order. She's a little lady and a beauty. I finally told my son, "O.K., enough is enough. Five children, my son, is more than enough."

Again I come to God thanking him once again for my handsome, wonderful sonny. Yes, he's my sonny and one of my best friends. God's graces and mercy have truly brought him through.

Chapter XI

FRIENDS, JOBS, CHURCHES AND PASTORS

Top left: Sally, me, Earlene. After Church in LA, friends for over *50* years. Mattie (friend) over *50* years. Gladys (friend) over *50* years. Leon, Gladys' husband. Earl and Barbara from Oakland at David's &

Pilar's wedding. Barbara (at work friend). Lower left: (friend) over *50* years Linnie. Her son Darryl. Linne and husband John meet on Grego ry's graduation day.

Top: RC & Cecilia Burch, friends for over 50 years. Cecilia. Irma (Friend). Mattie, me, Darlene Shanks friends. Darlene. Mattie and Ruth. Sophia Taylor (Allstate). Florece (LAUSD). Sondra Odom (Sup., LAUSD).

Lower left: Beverly Calhoun (Allstate), Malcolm, Jason, Malinda, Ron nie (Allstate). Bishop Joseph (Evangelist Norma Moseley, LAUSD)

Top Left: Rita Humes and me. LAUSD. Cooking hot water corn- bread for potluck.
Top Right: My adopted son, Glen Nelson, doing his karate. Ann Tyson, friend, LAUSD.
Evelyn White, LAUSD, friend. Gwen Ayers, LAUSD, friend. Lower left: me, Nahid
Vakihian, Rosa, Social Services friends. Lacrecia, Social Services friend. Renee Brown,
Denise, Jackquelyn Brewer, Social Services friends. Bottom row: Lisa and husband Eric,
Social services. Ariel (husband) and Laurie (adopted daughter), Social services. Lower
right: Judy Henneman, Social services friend.

Top left: Lacretia and Jacquelyn (social services). Husband Charles and Jacquelyn, social services. LaSurer, social services. Debbie Lazan, social services. Denise Davidson, social service. Midred, Mitchell, and me. Retirement party, Oakland, Ca. Friends from Hollywood Accessories. Joe Anne Hayes, Supervisor, Hollywood Accessories. Randy Banks. Pastor Leroy-Haley. Lower left: Debbie Harris, Johnson Chapel AME Church. Diane Renee. Gail Alfried, social services.

My book would not be complete without acknowledging some special people and friends that have been a blessing to me and my children through good and difficult times. Also the various co-workers I've met and the wonderful supervisors and bosses that I've had. I can't possibly mention everyone, and certainly wouldn't want feelings hurt because a name is omitted. I will only mention a few.

There are friends like Earlene who I have known since elementary school. We have never had a disagreement or an unkind word to say to each other. We went to junior high and high school together were in various sports, also sang together in an awesome group. We were members of the same church and sang in the choir. We had one of the greatest choirs in Orange County. We went to parties together, got into trouble and on punishment at the same time and shared each others deepest secrets. Our parents totally trusted us together not realizing we would never tell on each other. This is the friend that came to my rescue when I was being mistreated by one of my husbands and moved us into her home. She stated that she was ready for him. I was her friend and I did not have to stay and take that abuse.

When Earlene moved to L.A. I was devastated. I sure missed her and I went to visit her as often as possible, but we eventually lost touch. One day I got a phone call from her and I was elated. We vowed never to lose contact again. I will love my friend forever.

Mattie, one of the best friends anyone could want, need or ever have. We have been friends for forty-one years and never have had a difference of opinion. Our children being around the same ages are also friends. We are as close as sisters and have genuine love for each other. We have been neighbors twice in Santa Ana. She had five children and I had two. I would be tired, and after I put my two children down for a nap, I would go over to

Mattie's, get on her couch to take a nap with the noise of all her children. We could never figure it out. Mattie always had goodies to eat and loved to cook and feed us. And we loved to eat, especially me. Sometimes we would just sit on the porch and watch the cars go by, talking for hours until it was time to cook dinner.

Again, I lost another friend to L.A. I was so hurt when Mattie told me she was moving to L.A. She said, "We will keep in touch. You know I will never forget you." However, we lost contact, but several years later I received a phone call. It was my friend. We started to laugh out of control and I wanted to cry. She explained that she had gotten Aunt Connie's phone number from information and that she took a chance on her living at the same address. "You can't get away from me. And we will never lose contact again." We exchanged addresses and phone numbers and that same week I was on the freeway going to visit my friend.

Whenever I go to visit her, she tells me to sit or lie down and tell her what I want to eat. "I don't want you to do anything but rest." She has always spoiled me. I would eat until I almost burst and then we would talk about all the good old days, our children, men and grandchildren until late into the night. We don't talk everyday or every week. Sometimes once a month, but we both know where we stand as friends. There is nothing I would not do for my friend and she has the same feelings for me. We really have fun when we travel together. We went to Seattle, Washington to visit her son and she knew I was afraid to fly. I talked all the way there when finally I said, "Mattie, how much longer?" She replied, "We just landed, now Dorothy, just calm down." We still laugh about that day. Mattie, friends till death do us part.

Gladys, another dear friend, came to Santa Ana from Laguna Beach in the 50's. I met Gladys at a teenage hangout at a school named Franklin

Elementary. She left Santa Ana in 1960, married and moved to San Diego. But this did not stop our friendship. She bonded with my two daughters, becoming their aunt and spoiled them with many beautiful gifts.

Gladys had six children by Leon, my sister-in-law Jean's brother. In 1993, she lost her oldest son to cancer. Gladys has been married for 40 years and still lives in San Diego. She currently has 13 grandchildren and two great, grand-children. I lost contact with Gladys for approximately 10 years and reunited one day when she was visiting our sister-in-law Jean in Los Angeles. We immediately exchanged telephone numbers and promised to stay in touch with each other. To this day we have kept that promise. I can always count on Gladys's friendship and support in every situation. We are sisters in Christ, sisters forever.

And then there was Linnie, a wonderful, sincere friend that I meet in the 60's, she moved to Orange County from Arkansas. We bonded as friends right away. I knew we were going to be good friends, both of us being from the South and Arkansas. What a coincidence. We became each other's right hand. Sure, we had other friends but we were closer than any sister could ever be. Linnie met and married one of our school friends from Santa Ana and they had three wonderful sons. She had her oldest son Darryl when she arrived. One day my friend told me that she and her family were moving to Arizona, it was work related. Her husband had been transferred. We were both sadden by this and she was gone. Eventually they moved back and we both were very happy, but I was moving to L.A. so we said our goodbyes again.

Linnie and her husband separated and she moved back to Arkansas. We called each other as much as possible. One day I received a call from her stating that she was moving to L.A. She had a sister that lived in the same city as I and I kept in touch with her to see when she would be arriving.

One day to my happiest surprise she was calling to tell me that she was on her way over and wanted directions to my house. Fifteen minutes later she was at my door. We were both so happy to see each other, we had so much catching up to do. And that we did. On the day of my son's graduation, Linnie met her future husband John and they are now happily married Christians with a beautiful relationship, and home in Carson. We don't talk every day or every week, but we talk because you see, we are friends forever, and ever.

Barbara moved to Santa Ana from Fresno in the 60's. She dated one of my brothers-in-law for a while and she and I became friends. She was also related to Jr. We babysit for each other; her daughter was like my own child. Barbara loved her music especially on the weekend. She would gather all the children together when we were visiting, blast her record player. "Say it loud! I'm black and I'm proud." She would have my son doing the camel walk. She later had a son. We did a lot of fun things together.

Barbara and her mother Daisy were friends first, then mother and daughter. All of the young people loved Daisy. We thought she was so cool. Daisy and Barbara later moved to Oakland. Another friend moving, what is this? Barbara and I continue to keep in touch and visit each other when possible. She is with a wonderful man named Earl who is like a brother to me. When I go to visit, he and Barbara make sure I have everything to make me feel at home and comfortable.

Every year in April on my birthday, I receive a card or a phone call from my friend. Every year in March on her birthday I forget her birthday. I get a call from her asking, "What day is this?" And I start screaming, "Barbara, not again, oh my God, not again! I forgot your birthday! I promise I want forget next year. I am going to write it down." And I did write it down, but what I did with it I don't know. Finally my daughter Pamela said,

"Mom, I can't believe you forget every year. I would be so embarrassed." I have gotten much better with my calls and cards, and I will treasure this friend forever.

I have many other friends: Dorothy and Cecilia, sisters; Doris, and Sally; Johnnie, Willie and Jimmy, Joe; Noland, Darlene and Ruth. I could go on and on page after page, and these are just some of my homies from the hood in Santa Ana. At various companies where I have worked, I have met and become friends with many other people.

Insurance Companies

At an insurance company there was Sophia. I loved her. She was one of the best friends I've ever had. She saw no colors and liked you for you. One day Sophia told me, "Dottie, I really admire you. I don't know how you do it with four children. Work all day, go home, cook, help your children with homework, catch the bus to work, continue to smile all the time and keep your sanity." I told her that I pray a lot and have good friends like her for mental support. She was wonderful to me and my children and did as much as she possibly could for me financially. My children loved her and she loved them.

When my car broke down, she went to her husband and discussed helping me to buy a car and pay them back in monthly payments. He agreed, so we went car hunting. They bought me a Mazda. Sometimes it was difficult to make the payment but I would get the money together and take it to her. She would ask, "Can you afford to pay this month?" I would lie and say sure, but she could read me so well, as good friends can, and would say, "Keep it this month and buy the children something special."

Every Christmas she and her husband would come over with a car full of gifts for my children including coats. Our company relocated and

Sophia and I were assigned to different locations. We kept in touch as much as possible and soon lost contact. She has two sons and lives in the Valley. I will someday reunite with my dear friend, she will forever be in my thoughts and heart.

On Wilshire Boulevard, where Sophia and I were working, there was a special adjuster with whom I worked, Mr. Sydel. He had compassion and concern for me and my children and would just shake his head when he would see me get off the bus every morning because our mazda needed a motor and I was back on the bus. He would say, "Dottie, I don't know how you do it. You are a strong woman." I would reply, "Mr. Sydel. I have to be for the sake of my children and I don't know any other way to be." He had a special Volkswagon car that he was working on as a hobby for years. When we were leaving work one evening he said, "Dottie, tomorrow I have a surprise for you so please don't be absent." I had no idea what he was up to. I could barely sleep.

The next day I was at work earlier than ever and to my surprise, his son had driven the V.W. that his dad had been working on to work. He had all the papers and gave them to me. I could only stand there with my mouth open. I said, "Mr. Sydel, I cannot take your car. This is your pride and joy." He said, "If you don't take it my feelings will be hurt." His son said that Mr. Sydel truly wanted me to have it. "He talks about you all the time, how he admire you. It still needs little minor things but nothing serious."

I started to cry and went and gave him a big hug and kiss. He said the car would last me a little while until I could afford something else. What a guy. I will never ever forget Mr. Sydel. How can I?

Ardel was also on Wilshire with us. She was like a daughter to me, young and sowing her wild oats. She could sing beautifully, so one year, for the Christmas program, the manager wanted us to form a group to sing Christmas carols. Ardel sang lead on several songs and the manager was impressed. This went on every year after that. He was a wonderful man and we all loved him.

At this same company I met Beverly. She was like a little sister to me. We rode together, had lunch together, went shopping and did many other things. She was a special friend and we had each other's back.

Cathy was special. She was a seamstress and made my girls formal dresses to model. They were going to modeling school and needed these special dresses. Cathy told me, "Dottie, I'll make the dresses for the girls. Just buy the material and come over for the fitting. I won't charge you a dime. I know you are a single parent trying to make it." I was so grateful and will forever be thankful to my friend Cathy.

Malinda and Ronnie Gossett, husband and wife, true friends forever. Malinda worked at the insurance company. We lived about a mile from each other and worked in Marina Del Rey. We would carpool together and would always run late leaving in the morning, but she always got us to work on time. What does that tell you? She and her husband were always there for me and my family. They are my son's godparents. They have two sons of their own, who are wonderful sons. We became like family, much closer than friends. I was older than this couple, but it never seemed to bother them at all. I was Dottie, their friend.

On one occasion I was over to their house very depressed, sharing some things with my friend about how I needed to get out of my relationship. I didn't quite know how to word it. She said, "Dottie, when you get home this evening, tell your husband that this marriage is not working out and that you want out. You want a divorce." Well, I did what she suggested and all hell broke loose. Later that evening all my children and I were at her door, bag and baggage. What could my friend do but let us in? She asked what happened and I told her that I ran it down to my husband like we had discussed. We had the biggest fight ever and he put us out. Malinda and I just laughed for hours after the shock wore off. Malinda said, "As long as I live, I will never give anyone else any advice!" Then we laughed some more. When Ronnie got home, she explained what had happened and he said, "Well, we just have to make room for them." Who could have asked for such marvelous friends as the Gossett's?

Los Angeles Unified School District (LAUSD)

After working at Allstate, I went to work at the Los Angeles Unified School District. Again, God had more rams in the bushes. I met Florece, Ann, Norma and her husband Elder Moseley, who was truly a blessing to my family. Elder Moseley taught me many things about God. He told me that God couldn't use a coward; he wanted strong dedicated people to spread his word. He taught me to have faith and to believe in myself. I thank God over and over again for putting Norma and Elder Moseley in my life. Norma was a strong woman who totally supported her husband. I loved Norma; she was always so quiet until she got started talking about the goodness of God. Then she was like thunder.

I was in a bad situation at home and Elder felt the torment that I was going through. He told me, "Dottie, you are in a situation where you either have to get out of it or deal with it using the word of God. God doesn't want or ask anyone to stay in a situation like this. I will continue to lift you and your children up." I went to Bible study held at the Moseley's home once a week. Sometimes I went to their church. We continue to be friends, even though we don't talk as often as we could or should, but I love them and I know they love me.

I met Florece before the Moseleys. In fact, she introduced us. Florece and I worked in the same department and we became friends right away. She was so knowledgeable and liked by everyone. She taught me a lot and I asked her question after question. She would assure me that it was okay to keep asking the same questions over and over. We started trusting each other with small talk at first, and then with more personal things. She had my back and I had hers. We exchanged telephone numbers and addresses.

Florece and I would have lunch together and go to the garment district. We stayed in trouble at the garment district. Florece was there for me through my marital problems and children problems. I was there for her through her boyfriend and children problems. I kept Florece laughing because I could imitate almost anyone. Her friendship was genuine and real and we continue to keep in touch. Ella Mosley was the supervisor, the best in the world. I was only a part time sub, but she kept me working full time, what an awesome lady.

I got really close to Rita and Glenn at the west office. I loved to make people laugh because that made me happy, and I kept them laughing. They all were great friends to me and I loved them. We promised to keep in touch forever. Glenn was like a son to me. There were other friends at this office, and I will never forget any of them. My supervisor, Sandra and I were super close, she was also awesome. Some of the co-workers thought she favored me, we laughed because we knew the answer to that.

Ann and I also became friends. Her daughter has a son making Ann a proud grandmother. She had me over for dinner often, her husband was a great cook and was very nice to me. It was always a pleasure to go to her house. Her husband would cook thick, juicy T-bone steaks, have salad, corn-on-the-cob and fresh bread. Of course it was a pleasure to visit my friend's house. When I got up from the table, all I wanted was a nice nap.

Ann always bought good lunches to work and shared with me. I was happy to see those lunches every day.

I was also a good friend to Ann. I helped her get all kinds of credit cards. One day when she came to visit me in Santa Ana, I was sharing with her how to obtain another credit card. Ann said, "Dottie, don't tell me about another credit card. Keep it to yourself. I don't want to see another card that has me enslaved. I gave all those cards back to the devil." I laughed so hard unitl I was crying. Ann was also an excellent comedian. Love you, Ann.

Orange County Social Services

I've met some wonderful people and friends at the County of Orange Social Services. West building was the office it all started for me. I had the pleasure of meeting and becoming Laurie's second mom. I had only been there a month and she came on board and chose to sit with me and have me to train her. I told her that this would be a challenge because I was new, but she became my shadow and I her mom. She got married and moved to another state, but I am still Mom to her and her husband, Ariel.

I also met friends like Rosa and her family, Denise, Debbie, Lisa and many more. During my training days, some of the young girls took me to Bobby McGee's for my birthday. I will never forget that night. I had never heard of this place. We sat down and they insisted that I have a glass of white or red wine. I didn't know which one to order so they ordered for me. When the music started, I almost jumped out of my skin it was so loud. Of course, I played it off and continued sipping my wine and eating dinner. I was old enough to be their mother, but it didn't seem to bother them. We were friends.

Nahid is very special. She has been like a wonderful daughter. She has supported me through family and financial situations. We were and still are best friends. I've met her family, and had dinner in her home. She has two wonderful children. Her husband's name is Mostafa, but I always call him Mo. Nahid and her husband have helped me many times financially whenever they could. She continues to love and support me. I have been invited on several occasions to come and live with them by my daughter Nahid. We continue to love, respect and support each other.

I continue to meet wonderful and sincere friends at SSA. Each office that I have worked at, I have met wonderful, unforgettable people. I was always closer to the younger workers rather than workers in my age group. Most of them think of me as Mom and friend. Sometimes they would weigh me down with their deep secrets and problems. Of course, they were not aware of the weight. I never told them but sometimes their intimate discussions would make me blush and take a deep breath. I would throw up my hands and just laugh.

Then I started to throw the ball back in to their court, weighing them down with my problems, hoping this would take their minds off their own problems. It worked. They all started trying to help solve Dottie's problems. Believe it or not, some of their solutions were fantastic and worked. My children were not jealous of so many adopted daughters; they felt honored that all these young people chose their mom. If it bothered them, they never told me. They liked my friends and, frankly, this kept me young. I would remind them, "Remember, I'm much older than all of you and I don't want to go every place you go or do everything you do." They would say, "Oh, we don't want to hear about your age, Mama Dottie."

One night two of my young friends, Nahid and Rosa, came over with food and tequila so we could have a good old mother-daughter talk. They had me drinking shooters and not being a drinker, those shooters got to me. When they got ready to leave for home after a couple of hours,

I couldn't even see them leaving. My head was throbbing and the room was going around and around. I never tried that again and they teased me about that night for months. I was so worried about them getting home but couldn't even call their house because I couldn't find my telephone! Shooters are not for everyone, especially Mama Dottie.

Another special friend I had was Cotie. We started as friends, then became like mother and daughter. She came to work at the Metro office and we started eating lunch together and became friends. Cotie was so much like a daughter that I thanked her mom for sharing her. When Cotie got married and her friend was giving her a bridal shower, she called for my address and didn't say I hope you can come, she said, "I expect you to be there. If you don't also come to my wedding I will be upset and hurt." Cotie married a wonderful young man. Of course I went to the shower and wedding.

I also had a wonderful supervisor at this office My Phueng, taught me so much, she called me Hot Mama. Why I have no idea, when I asked she simply said she bet I was a hot mama in my younger years.

Renee is a working evangelist. She is strong in her commitment to Christ. She is my wonderful praying friend and sister in Christ. Being younger than my youngest child, it did not bother her, It doesn't matter about the age. You are my friend and I love you. She is one of my prayer partners at work, standing in the gap for my finances, children, job and, of course, a husband for me. She keeps me covered with the blood of Jesus. Renee is always calm, easy going and in tune with God. If Renee sees me with a long face, she asks what's wrong. I tell her and she would tell me not to worry. I could feel her prayers. She has a wonderful husband, Wallace, and two very good looking sons. Thank you, Renee, for all your support, love and prayers.

Lacretia was in my unit at ARC. We got to be friends right away. She was wonderful to me and whenever I got stuck on something, she was there to help me. We also ate lunch together everyday. Whenever you saw me, you would see Lacretia. I met her wonderful family and they were just as wonderful as she was. I also had the pleasure of meeting her handsome fianceé. She was a wonderful listener, when I needed to vent my frustrations, and a supporter when I needed support. I thanked her mom for sharing her wonderful daughter. I thanked Lacretia for being my sincere friend.

My cool, calm and patient friend, Jackie, helps keep me in line and calm. She tells me, "O.K., calm down and don't worry about it." I've also had the pleasure of meeting her beautiful family. Jackie is from a strong praying family; her dad is a minister. Again, Jackie never looked at my age, she just saw me as her friend, and I feel the same about her. There is not a day that goes by that Jackie does not call and say good morning and how are you doing this morning. One thing impressed me above all; I was worried about a bill with a balance of $3000.00. She said, "Dottie, if I had the money, I would gladly give it to you. Not loan, give." I was touched. She has a wonderful husband, Charles, and two wonderful children.

Also remembering being transferred to a new unit in the same building and Judy Henneman was my cubical partner. She and I became friends. Judy was so knowledgeable and helpful. She was a great worker and finished her work quickly. She always asked if she could help me with anything. I was touched. Judy was tough, meaning she knew her stuff and didn't allow anyone to bother me. I told her I was writing a book and asked if I could mention her in my book. She said, "Dottie, I would be honored." Judy's boyfriend made her lunch every day. It was huge and healthy. She started sharing her lunch with me, and when she mentioned it to her boyfriend, I swear it got bigger. Judy was promoted back to supervisor and left the unit. I was so sad to see her go. My loss and management's gain. Thank you, Judy, my friend.

I had the pleasure of meeting Lasure at one of Social Services' offices. She was so friendly and only there for a short time. I ran into her again at another office and we became friends. I could go into her office, of course on my breaks, and vent about anything. I considered her wise and knowledgeable We had even considered opening a business together at one time. I would go into her office and make her laugh and then we would share the goodness of God, reminding each other to keep God first in our everyday living. Thanks and love to Lasure, my sister in Christ.

People like Adele made a difference in my life. Several days before my birthday I made the statement to one of my co-workers that I wish someone would buy me some Victoria Secret for my birthday. I had said that I did not own any and I loved it. The next day on my desk was a set of body spray and lotion by Victoria Secret from Adele. This made my day. Ronnie Gomez also gave me a beautiful set. Not only did these young ladies give me gifts, they gave me respect and love.

Other Special Friends

I met Diane one evening when she and her husband, who was my brother's best friend, came to visit. She was quiet and pleasant. I liked her right away. She and I had a lot in common and we also found out that our birthdays were a day apart. When they left that evening I told Jr. that I liked her, that she was very sweet. We continue to keep in touch and have become very good friends. We talk at least once or twice a week. She is like a little sister. She lost her husband in 1995 and all of us were devastated. Since his death, we have become even closer. Diane. Forever friends.

Mildred and I worked together at an auto accessories company in Compton. I realized after several conversations, she and I had a lot in common: age and children. I also noticed that Mildred was a Christian woman and kept to herself. Everyone knew and liked her and they called her Sister Mitchell. She and I talked a lot. One day she invited me to visit her church. I went one Sunday and enjoyed it so much that I continued to go for awhile. Finally I joined and started singing in the choir. They have an awesome director of music. The pastor was not only a powerful preacher, he became a wonderful friend. I was impressed with his friendship and concern for all the youth. Mildred and I became sisters in Christ. She would encourage and support me in everything, especially when I sang. Her family is like my family. Mildred's three beautiful daughters are like my very own nieces. I thank Mildred for her inspiration, her spiritual advice and most of all her prayers.

One of the most awesome, wonderful supervisors was at this same company. M.D., he was the "man," and his choice words was "Move your ass." The quota had to be met and then the party was on. Everyone loved him until month end. He hated my situation at home and was wonderful to me.

Randy was not only a co-worker at the same accessories company, he was and still is a dear friend and brother. He was wonderful to me and loved my daughter Deborah like his own. If Randy would get upset with me, he would tell me off in a nice brotherly way and be done with it. Then we would hug and make up. He would tell me, sometimes, "You make me so angry when you say, 'Don't be ignorant, Randy', but you know I love the hell out of you." Randy was always there for me with support and understanding and hated what I was going through at home. He would tell me also to call him if I ever needed him. Love you, Randy, my brother.

Cadie was another special friend that hated the way Mister treated me. She often told me that he should not be married to me. "I would love to just go over there one day and tell him off, good old-fashioned style in my own way. Then he would leave you alone. You don't deserve this."

Debbie Harris and I met at church in Santa Ana and became friends right away. She and I talked often, she told me, "You know that I support you in writing your book. Anything you need, please let me know."

I also met another friend Gail who was a co-worker at one of SSA's offices. We sat across from each other and one day started sharing different things. She told me how she loved angels which was one of my hobbies too, collecting angels. So right away we had something in common. We have been friends ever since, spending weekends and going on outings. I've had the pleasure of also meeting some of her wonderful family. Gail is a special friend. She was delighted when I told her I was going to mention her in my book.

As you can see, I have wonderful friends from many years ago to the present. I was sharing this with my friend Renee one day and I told her that I don't know what has happened to all of my old friends. We were so close once upon a time and now some of them are in their own world. Some are caught up in their men, others on material things they have acquired. I guess I don't fit in with some of their present lifestyles or financial status. I know that with some of them I was a more sincere friend than they were to me, but I know I am a child of God and that makes me a special somebody. She explained that the answer to that was time. There is a time and a season for everything including friendships. You are still their friend and they are still yours.

After Jr. died I had an appointment with my orthodontist. I was sitting there in the chair so down and sad that the office manager came over and asked me what was wrong. I told her and started to cry, then she started to cry. I explained that I knew that I still owed a lot of money, but to be honest I didn't have any money right now. She said not to worry about my bill. It is paid in full. Thank you, Lauren. I will never forget you or my orthodontist.

I haved worked in some wonderful churches with wonderful pastors., members and awesome choirs. Rev. Haley was one of those special pastors who I loved to hear bring the message. I always knew when the Holy Spirit hit him. He loved the choir and loved to hear me sing "Yes, Lord."

He had a beautiful wife that always made me feel welcome and loved. She was always smiling. When I moved away and could not attend regularly, I would go to visit whenever possible. She would greet me with smiles and hugs, always asking, "Where have you been?" She would say how much I was missed. Hearing this made my day. I felt special and loved.

One of Rev. Haley's sons Nate was also special to me, supporting me whenever I sang or telling me how pretty I looked. Now coming from a young man, that was special. One day he told me to look up the word beautiful in the dictionary. "That is you," he said. I blushed and thanked him and thought to myself, God does keep his children beautiful regardless of the age. This same son is now a great pastor of his own church.

One year Mrs. Hooperland asked me if I would do a concert at United Christian M.B.C. I was honored and consented. It was a great day for me. The spirit was high in the church and my family and friends were there from San Diego to Oakland, totally supporting me. My grandmother and aunt were in the front row and that made it more special than ever. I was so full that I could barely sing, but I sang to the glory of God. God got all the praise and honor for that concert. Rev. Haley was proud of me and was smiling through the entire concert.

There is another pastor who touched my heart. He was new to Johnson Chapel A.M.E. in Santa Ana. He was young and full of fire and I loved that. I felt comfortable talking to him from the first day. He was like a son. I was going through some financial burdens that were really weighing me down and one Sunday after church he read me and asked if something was wrong. I told him I would call him one day and tell him about it. I called and made an appointment and explained my situation. He said, "I am here to help you and I will." I was asked to call him back the next day, when I called. He asked me to come to the church office. By the time I left the office, I was blessed and started to cry, thanking God all the way home. I told Pastor Kyler that I would pay it back as soon as I could. He said not to worry about it. "If you try to pay it back, that will put you in a bigger financial burden. This is what we are here for. We love you. Now go home and stop worrying." Pastor Kyler, I love you. Thank you for being a concerned pastor, but most of all for being my friend.

I moved to Corona in 1996 and was looking for a closer church to visit. My cousin Kim invited me to go to church with her one Sunday. She said, "It's a small church but I'm sure you will like it." I went and she was right. It was on fire for the Lord. There were two pastors, but the church was one big family. One pastor preached and the next Sunday, the other pastor preached. They both are great pastors. The church is mixed ethnically: black, white, brown, red, yellow, rich or poor. All were welcome to come and be fed. I joined as a watch member and guess where I worked? Yes, the choir, of course.

Left top: Robert, Deborah's son. Next row: Christopher, Dönte, Gregory's children. Far right; Jushona, Sue's daughter. Bottom: Pam's daughter, Bänka

I told you I had something to say. This is almost my whole story. My grandchildren came to me and asked, "Are you going to say anything about us?" A book would not be a complete book without a grandmother prais ing her grandchildren.

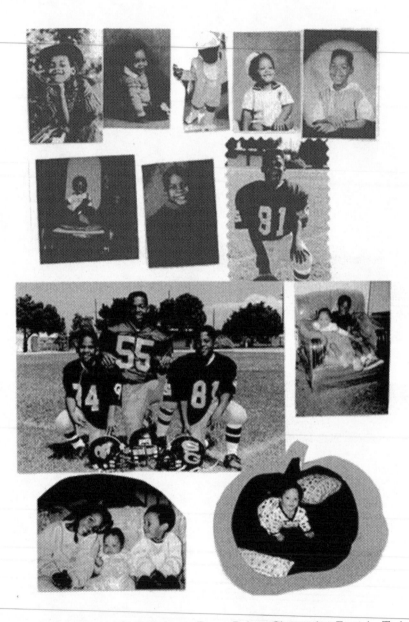

Left top: Banka. Center: 3 football players, Donte, Robert, Chris topher. Far right: Taylor, Aaron (Greg's kids). Bottom: Tiffany, Taylor, Aaron. Lower right: baby Taylor

Grandchildren
Top left: Christopher, Dönte, Aaron. Center: Tiffany, Taylor. Right:
Tiffany, Christopher, Robert, Aaron, Dönte, Taylor

Robert: fourteen years old, self-taught computer whiz, intelligent, and loves all of his cousins, but sometimes they get on his nerves.

Christopher: ten years old, serious and concerned, especially about his little brother, very wise for his age.

B'anka: nine years old, princess, scholar, dramatic, she can make a dance out of any record given to her.

D'onte: scholar and comedian, gets tired of everyone telling him that he looks just like his grandmother, he tells them, "I look just like D'onte", he is the brother of Christopher.

Tiffany: five years old, wants you to define everything, always asking what does that mean?

Aaron: three years old, has an answer for everything, a smart answer, he is the brother of Tiffany, D'onte, and Christopher.

Taylor: my newly born beautiful and smart-not much to say yet, but just wait.

These are my beautiful and wonderful grandchildren.

AFTERWORD

One evening in November of 1997, I was talking to my brother on the phone. I asked if he had thought of, or written anything for my book. He got really quiet. His voice suddenly cracked. He said, "Dorothy, it's really hard for me to go back to that day. I don't like to even think about that horrible day." At that moment, he started to cry. I said, "William, the way you are acting and keep putting it off day after day, you make me think you are hiding something, as if you are going to say it was Daddy." Still crying he said in a very low voice, "It was, it was Daddy. He did it. He killed mother and Joyce. It was Daddy that I saw running from the house into the field. When he turned around to look back our eyes met. I have been terrified ever since that day. I surpressed everything until today." I screamed and started to cry. I threw the phone down and cried out of control for at least five minutes. When I finally picked up the phone, my brother was still crying. I said don't cry, little brother, now you can start healing. You have held this in for fifty years. He said, "I don't want to talk about it anymore tonight," and we said goodbye.

My mind went back to something my cousin Gerline had told me. She said the day of Mother's murder, she and her boyfriend were sitting on the porch of my great grandmother Molly's house and they saw Daddy walking down the road looking up at the hot sun in a daze. As he got closer, they could see he was covered with blood. He called to her boyfriend to come to him, that he wanted to ask him something. He proceeded to ask him, "Does Lorene go with S.W.?" Gerline's boyfriend's reply was, "No, what is wrong with you?" Daddy continued saying that Lorene and Joyce were dead and walked off still looking up at the sun as if he had lost his mind. Gerline told this to me also this year.

I called my sister after William hung up and told her what had happened and the crying started all over again. She said, "But, Dorothy, this does not surprise me. You know we have always suspected Daddy, but no one ever wanted to talk to us about what happened." Up to this point, we had been giving our dad the benefit of doubt saying, maybe he got to the house after the fact and tried to help mother and Joyce; or he was outside and saw the whole thing; or he hired the killer and came by to see if it had been done. Finally there were no more maybe's and we were quiet for at least a minute to collect our thoughts, because in our hearts we had believed that it was him all along. Why then on his death bed did he continue to lie? It was a white man that was angry with me and did not like me, when he was telling this story to us. We looked at each other in disbelief and it is still unbelievable. We both agreed that the three of us should now try to get on with our lives. The next day I called my brother to see if he was o.k. He said that he felt a lot better but could not sleep all night. William said that all of his life he had resented Daddy and had even said that he had one day thought about killing him, but thought how it would hurt all of us. He said he was afraid that Daddy was going to come after him and kill him because Daddy knew that he had seen him. That eye contact had put the fear in him. Sometimes he thought he was losing his mind. He tried to forget and almost had until I started to write my book. "I got scared all over again, even though Daddy was dead." I told him, "You are free, little brother. Now we have to pray for deliverance and healing."

My little ones growing up

COLLAGE

Top: Ruth and Adolph Roosevelt. Long time friends. Center: Gloria and Bloy Stiner. Regina's Mother and Father in Law and long time friends. Right: Cousin Connie and Maudie.

Bottom Left: Trina, Pam, Earlene. Jackie at concert. Doris Spencer. Alvin and Vickie (Maxine's daughter and boyfriend). Earl and Mrs. Duffey. Rickie, Pan, Alvin.

Top left: God Children: Wendy and Willie Horne. Center: Mother and Bro. Sims Jordon (prayer partners and friend). Top right: Yvonne, me. Rossie Michael, Rosy.

Top left: Bro William and me (David's marriage). Top right; Joe Mc Dade and me. Jerline, Aunt Nellie. Regina, Mama Carrie, Pam, Pee wee, Rachelle, Debbie, Dwayne. William, Jessie (cousin). Hazel and Grace Gates (friends) from Santa Ana. Easter Group: Sja, me, Pam, Debbie, Vicki. Right borrom: Rozita, Maudie, Jessie, Connie, me.

Top left: Anthony, Pam, Greg, William. Me and John (dancing). Lori and Greg (Tiffany, Aaron, and Taylor's mom). Center: Anthony, Regina, Yvonne. Gladys, Trina. William and Marlyn (party in Carson). Gregory and Sja (Christpher and Donte's mom). Rozita and Rossie Mom. Alvin and Pam.

Printed in the United States
By Bookmasters